D0760680

These are **uncorrected page proofs**.
No part of these proofs may be
reproduced without the written
permission of Harvard University Press.
Not for sale.

THE TEMPLE OF JERUSALEM
By Simon Goldhill
Publication Date: March 2005
Price: $19.95
ISBN: 0-674-01797-8
208 pages, 25 halftones, 9 line illustrations
Harvard University Press

For more information, please contact:
Mary Kate Maco
Publicity Director
Phone 617.495.4713
Fax 617.349.5244
mary_kate_maco@harvard.edu

Visit our Web site
www.hup.harvard.edu

WONDERS OF THE WORLD

THE TEMPLE OF JERUSALEM

THE TEMPLE OF JERUSALEM

SIMON GOLDHILL

HARVARD UNIVERSITY PRESS

Cambridge, Massachusetts

2005

First published in the United Kingdom in 2004 by
Profile Books Ltd
58A Hatton Garden
London ECIN 8LX

Library of Congress Cataloging-in-Publication Data
Goldhill, Simon.
The Temple of Jerusalem / Simon Goldhill.
p. cm.
Includes bibliographical references (p.) and index.
ISBN 0-674-01797-8 (alk. paper)
1. Temple of Jerusalem—History. I. Title.
DS109.3.G65 2005   296.4'91—dc22   2004054307

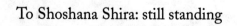

To Shoshana Shira: still standing

CONTENTS

I

··

A MONUMENT OF THE
IMAGINATION

DESTROYED MAGNIFICENCE

On the morning of 28 August AD 70, the Roman supreme
military commander Titus called together his generals for a
last briefing before the final assault on Jerusalem. The campaign to crush the rebellion of the Jews of the province of
Judaea had stretched over three years, culminating in a grim
five-month siege of Jerusalem itself. Today was the day for
the storming of the city. The question for discussion,
however, was the fate of the Temple of the Jews. The Temple
dominated the city and the surrounding countryside. It was
the largest and most awe-inspiring religious monument in
the world. It glittered with gold and shining white stone, and
its magnificence staggered even the hard-nosed Titus, the
future Emperor of Rome. It was also the central, symbolic
stronghold of the Jews.

The best-known version of what happened next is given
to us by Josephus, the historian who wrote from the very particular position of being a former Jewish leader now spon-
sored by the Roman authorities to produce the official
history of the Jewish war. He tells us that the generals
advised the pragmatic military option, as generals predictably

do. The Jews would never stop rebelling while the Temple stood as a focus for political and religious activity. So, destroy it! But Titus took a different viewpoint. He would never burn so impressive a work, he declared: 'The loss would be for Rome. Its continuing existence will be a glory of the Empire.' The generals were ordered to preserve the Temple.

But not everything can go according to plan in war. The Jews fought with desperate ferocity, and in the battle a Roman soldier threw a firebrand through one of the low golden doors of the Temple. The cedarwood furnishings quickly caught fire, the Roman soldiers lost control and the sack of Jerusalem turned into a riot of violence, looting and destruction. Whether we trust Josephus' account or not, the end result is clear enough. This wonder of the ancient world was burnt to the ground.

When the fighting was over, the Romans, ever thorough, completely ploughed over the site. So thorough were they in fact that not one stone or artefact from the sacred building of the Temple itself has survived to the modern era. Among the other rich spoils, Titus took the Temple's famous seven-branched golden candelabrum back to Rome, where it was paraded in triumph before the citizens, a victory celebration recorded for posterity on the Arch of Titus. The Temple can now be pictured only in the mind's eye, and this small image from the inside of Titus' memorial has made the Arch a necessary stop for tourists to Rome in a way that the emperor could never have expected. What was meant to be a monument to Titus' everlasting military glory has become an icon of the enduring symbolic power of the destroyed Temple of the Jews.

The temple Titus destroyed had been built by Herod and

1. Roman soldiers with the holy candelabrum from the Temple,
from the Arch of Titus, in Rome.

[3]

stood for less than ninety years. Its lavish decorations had been finally finished only six years before their destruction. Herod is a familiar figure from the Christian Gospels – the murderous, stupid and vain tyrant who ordered the Massacre of the Innocents. He was king over the Jews, but he ruled what was actually a province of the Roman Empire only by permission of the Roman state. (It was typical of the Roman Empire in this period to govern through local potentates.) The construction of the Temple was the most grandiose act of self-promotion, the capstone of a building programme throughout the kingdom, designed to proclaim Herod a famous and popular man of power for future generations to admire. In a sense, it worked rather well. It is only because he built the Temple that this unpopular and mistrusted king is known today as Herod the Great.

The scale of the project is, even today, simply staggering. For the Temple he first constructed a massive earth and rock platform, 144,000 square metres in area – the size of twelve football pitches – and thirty-two metres high. This was held in place by four huge stone retaining walls, which are in themselves a quite remarkable feat of engineering. One of these retaining walls, the Western, has become the most recognisable image of religious Jerusalem: the 'Wailing Wall'. For nearly 2,000 years Jews have gathered there to mourn the loss of the Temple and to pray – and from the earliest Christians to the newspapers of today, images of those in prayer at the Wall have proved an easy, ideologically charged way of representing 'the Jews'. The wall actually had no religious significance at all in Herod's time: where people now pray was no more than a road at the bottom of the wall which held up the platform on which the Temple stood. It was a

2. All images of the Jews at the Western Wall are highly politicised. In 1890, the Jews can be shown as strange, Eastern, poor: very much the Other for the Victorian traveller.

[5]

3. But in about 1990, in the London newspaper the *Guardian*, the military presence, juxtaposed both to the ultra-orthodox worshipper and just visible at the back a visitor in modern dress, creates a different but equally ideologically-loaded image of contemporary Israel for the *Guardian* reader.

functional solution to the architectural problem of the platform, and not part of the Temple itself. But over time it has become invested with the deepest sanctity, a place of profound religious feelings.

This is absolutely typical of how people have come to care passionately about the Temple. The physical building may no longer exist, but both the site of the Temple and the idea of it have inspired men and women for generations – and have been fought over with matching intensity. The Temple takes shape in the minds of men. And there's the rub. The Temple is never just a destroyed building. It has become the most potent symbol of the human search for a lost ideal, an image of former greatness and greatness to come. It is an idea that has prompted struggle, brutal war between cultures and nations, and some of the most moving poetry and art of the Western tradition. A history of the Temple can never be merely an architectural record, nor just an account of religious rituals. We need a special sort of archaeology for this great building of the world, an archaeology that uncovers not so much rock and dust as the sedimented layers of human fantasy, politics and longing. This book will be a tour of this bizarre and wonderful history of an imagined building: it will take us from sex and politics in the Bible to the violence and romance of the Knights of the Crusades, from the myth and rituals of Freemasonry to the imperialism of Islamic warriors, from the fantasies of Victorian adventurers to the question of why barristers are called barristers …

FROM SOLOMON TO SALADIN TO SHARON

Herod's Temple itself replaced a former Temple which in

turn had replaced the first Temple built by Solomon. Three temples, three stories of destruction: this site in Jerusalem constantly evokes a multi-layered tale of memory and loss, ruin and reconstruction (which is one reason it has held such power over the imagination). According to the Hebrew Bible, Solomon was given the plans for the first Temple by King David, his father, and the Book of Kings describes in loving detail the wondrous construction of this centre of early Jewish religious and political life. This first, glorious Temple was destroyed by Nebuchadnezzar, King of Babylon, in 587 BC. The Israelites were forced into exile in Babylon: 'By the rivers of Babylon, I lay down and wept as I remembered thee, O Zion.' It was a crushing disaster, and a major break in the development of Judaism as well as in the history of the Israelite people; it also stimulated some of the most moving poetry of the Psalms and the Prophets, which in turn has led to some of the most beautiful music of the Western tradition from Thomas Tallis's *Lamentations of Jeremiah* to Bob Marley's 'Exodus' ('We're leaving Babylon …').

However, when the Persians under Cyrus the Great rose with stunning rapidity to defeat the Babylonians and to dominate the whole of Asia Minor (the Persian Empire was the first real empire in Western history), the Jews were given permission in 538 BC by an edict of Cyrus himself to return to Jerusalem and rebuild their Temple: Cyrus even promised 'foreign aid' to help with the building. The Persians, like so many imperial powers, were masterful at public relations and wanted to be welcomed as a liberating force. So, in theory at least, the Jews were free to go home. In practice, things were not quite so straightforward. Politics, administrative delays and general difficulties meant that the project to build the temple was not completed until 515 BC, under the Persian king Darius.

A shadowy figure called Zerubbabel was instrumental in the rebuilding project, and traditionally he gives his name to this replacement of Solomon's Temple. Zerubbabel's Temple always fell short of its great predecessor in the eyes of those who worshipped there. Squeezed between the glories of Solomon and the majesty of Herod, the temple of Zerubbabel has always been the poor relation. None the less, it stood for 500 years until Herod's Temple replaced it in 19 BC.

There are, then, three different buildings known as the Temple of Jerusalem: Solomon's, Zerubbabel's and Herod's. Over the course of its history, the site was invaded, desecrated and rededicated time and again in the wars which swept the region. The history of the Temple is one of constant conflict and of repeated new beginnings.

Indeed, Titus' destruction of Herod's Temple is itself only one more beginning in the life of the temple as an idea and image. It forms a fundamental moment in another new development to build a house of God: the beginning of Christianity. 'When Jesus came out of the Temple, one of his disciples said to him, "Look, Teacher, what wonderful stones and what wonderful buildings." And Jesus said to him, "Do you see these great buildings? There will not be left here one stone upon another that will not be thrown down"' (Mark 13). The Gospel of Mark was written shortly after the Roman sack of Jerusalem, so this prophecy is certainly historically pointed and would have powerfully resonated with its first readers. But when Jesus was asked for further explanation of his lapidary message, he gave an apocalyptic vision of the end of the world, which lends his words a far broader theological

[9]

impact. Indeed, in the Gospel of John, Jesus declares, 'Destroy this temple, and in three days I will raise it up again' (John 2). John and the disciples understand this to refer to Jesus himself, raised from the dead after three days. In some sense, for Christians Jesus himself becomes the Temple. The 'new Jerusalem', the 'new Temple' of Jesus, is a central image of Christianity, which opposes an everlasting divine Temple to an earthly temple, made and destroyed by the hands of men, and opposes the community of faithful Christians to the rituals of the Temple. For Christians, the destruction of the Temple heralds the triumph of Christianity.

This explains why the Christians treated the Temple Mount in the surprising way they did. Helena, the mother of the first Christian emperor, Constantine the Great, and herself an ardent Christian, was the first Christian member of the imperial family to visit Jerusalem. Constantine had initiated a building programme, headed by the Church of the Holy Sepulchre, built over what was claimed to be the tomb of Jesus; Helena directed the foundation of a series of monuments to memorialise Jesus' life and death in Jerusalem and Bethlehem. But all the Christian emperors left the Temple Mount – Herod's platform – deliberately undeveloped, although it was another crucial site in the life of Jesus: it was, after all, where he had taught and from where he had thrown out the money-changers. There was a temple of Jupiter which had been built on the platform by the Emperor Hadrian to make visible another crushing defeat of a Jewish revolt against the Empire. This was purposefully dismantled and the statues of the emperors were taken down too. This made the site wholly bare. For the Temple Mount had to be left as a field of desolation permanently to recall the wrongheaded rejection of Jesus by the Jews (a sort of negative building programme). For Helena and Constantine, as for many later theologians, the behaviour of the Jews was the cause of the destruction of the Temple. In this fully Christian history, the empty Temple Mount was to stand as a barren sign of the failure of Judaism.

Three hundred years later the Christians themselves came under the domination of new imperial rulers – the Muslims – who had a quite different sense of the importance of the Temple Mount. In 638 Caliph Omar conquered Jerusalem at the head of a Muslim army. He insisted that the Christian patriarch lead him to the Temple Mount – or Haram al-Sharif (in Arabic, 'Noble Sanctuary'). He found the site used as a rubbish dump. He forced the patriarch to crawl on his hands and knees through the refuse to punish him for insulting the holy sites of other religions and, according to one story at least, began to clean up the detritus with his own hands. Omar built a large rectangular wooden building, big enough for 3,000 men, in the middle of the Mount (where it was visited in 680 by the French bishop Arculf, who wrote one of the earliest traveller's accounts of visiting Muslim Jerusalem: 'crude work', he sniffed). In 691, however, Caliph Abd al-Malik erected in its place the stunningly beautiful Dome of the Rock, the Qubbat al-Sakhra, the glorious octagonal building now capped by a golden dome which still dominates the skyline of Jerusalem. This building houses the rock on which, it was said, Abraham bound Isaac for sacrifice; the same rock was believed to be the altar of Solomon's Temple, and it was where the prophet Mohammed rose from the earth on a winged steed to meet Abraham, Moses and Jesus in heaven, where he led them in prayers. The rock itself wanted to follow, and the print of Mohammed's foot where he pushed the rock back to earth is still to be seen on it today. The Dome of the Rock is a *mashhad*, a shrine for pilgrims (and not, strictly speaking, a mosque, although it is often called one). It was the first of a series of splendid buildings which still adorn the Haram al-Sharif. Islam recognises the prophetic tradition of Judaism and Christianity, but declares itself to transcend both. The Dome of the Rock visibly instantiates that transcendence: it is built on the traditions of those other religions, and is designed to soar magnificently – and symbolically – over the city of Jerusalem.

The Christian West responded slowly to the rise of Islam. The first Crusaders set out to win back Jerusalem more than 400 years later and, after particularly bloody and unpleasant fighting, in 1099 Jerusalem was once again ruled by Christians. A cross was placed on the Dome of the Rock, and for more than eighty years in the twelfth century the Dome became the Templum Domini, the Temple of Our Lord: a Christian temple. For the earlier Christians the empty site was an image of the triumph of Christianity; now the Muslim shrine, turned into a temple of the Christian God, played the same triumphant role. The Knights Templar (named, of course, precisely for the Temple), a religious and military order, took up residence on the Temple Mount and kept their horses in the Stables of Solomon. Churches in the shape of the *mashhad* were built all over Europe to celebrate this victory and, ironically enough, both Solomon's Temple and Herod's appear in Western art in the shape of the Dome of the Rock.

This Christian dominance, however, was brief. The great general Saladin won back Jerusalem for the Muslims, and

4. A medieval Christian miniature of Jerusalem at the time of the Crucifixion (the Crucifixion itself is represented at the apex of the picture) by an anonymous fifteenth-century Flemish artist. The temple appears anachronistically as the Dome of the Rock.

held it against Richard the Lionheart; once again the cross on the Dome was replaced with a crescent. By the sixteenth century Jerusalem was part of the Turkish Ottoman Empire. Suleiman the Magnificent not only rebuilt the walls and aqueducts of Jerusalem, but also decorated the Dome of the Rock with its beautiful blue and green Persian tiles. And Jerusalem, with the Islamic Temple Mount at its centre, remained part of the Ottoman Empire for over 300 years until 1917, when Allenby entered Jerusalem for the British forces – humbly, on foot, as he constructed the image of the moment of conquest with brilliant visual rhetoric – and the British Mandate took over. In 1948, the State of Israel was formed, and in 1967 Jerusalem, including the Temple Mount, came fully under Israeli governance following the Six Day War.

From the fourteenth century, however, despite long-running and difficult tensions between the Turkish Ottomans and the Arabs, the Temple Mount itself has been under the legal control of the Islamic authorities (the Waqf), and so it remains, even while Jerusalem is ruled by the Israelis. Entrance to it for many years was restricted to the Muslim faithful – although the occasional Western dare-devil traveller describes dressing up in disguise to steal a look at the sacred site. (One man, who published in 1816 under the pseudonym of Ali Bey el Abassi, described to an enthralled European public how he visited 'the shrine of the infidel' five times, disguised as a Muslim.) The Jews argued – and argue still – whether it is even allowable in religious law for Jews to step on it at all after the destruction: the problem is that anyone might enter the forbidden zone of the Holy of Holies by mistake. It is somewhat ironic, therefore, that the first

European to be granted official permission by the Ottoman authorities to visit the Temple Mount (in 1855) was Sir Moses Montefiore, the great Jewish philanthropist, who was also the first European allowed to buy property in Jerusalem. This permission was granted partly because of Britain's support of Turkey in the Crimean War, partly because Montefiore was an internationally famous diplomatic grandee of the British Empire. He visited by his usual method of transport, sedan chair, so it is unclear whether his feet touched the holy ground or not. The site was emptied and put under state guard for the potentially explosive trip. (Montefiore himself, however, seems to have been quite uninterested in the experience – just another formal duty, it seems – and scarcely mentions it in his diary of the tour. The Western Wall was much more moving to him.) Montefiore, however, was actually excommunicated by ultra-orthodox rabbis for making his visit. Who steps on to the Temple Mount – and how – has been a contentious issue of national politics for centuries. When the Israeli politician Ariel Sharon went to the site in 2000, an event which marked the beginning of the second intifada, it was this long history of zealously guarded space which filled every response to his visit with so much emotion.

Is there any other place in the world that has had such symbolic investment by so many people and which has been so fiercely fought over by individuals and empires? As a political and religious centre, it inevitably became the focus of war and social struggle, but, as a destroyed building, the space of its absence has attracted the hopes and aspirations of millions of people over the centuries, and continues to fuel the most intense feelings in the Middle East and beyond. This is what makes its history so compelling.

One particular thing should be clear from this brief overview: the history of the Temple is a history of clashing cultures. It is the clash of monotheistic Jewry with the surrounding tribes and religions, and with its own non-monotheistic elements; the clash of the Roman Empire and the rebellious Jews; the clash of militant Christians with Romans and with Jews; and it is the clash between the new religion of Islam and the traditions of Christianity and Judaism. Today we must add the clash between secularism and religion itself. These clashes are enacted in stories, in histories, in building programmes and in bloody wars: the Temple Mount is a place where the self-expression of different cultures is articulated in the most fervent manner. Fighting over Jerusalem is never just a military operation: there is always much more at stake. It hardly needs emphasising that this long history of cultural conflict continues to have a profound effect on the political, religious and intellectual lives of us all. The inheritance of these enduring conflicts is all too insistent in contemporary society.

Because of this inheritance, anyone discussing the Temple inevitably becomes drawn into national and religious history. For Jews, Christians and Muslims alike, to talk of the Temple means to take part in such history, and this history cannot be written without the Temple finding a place. There's a nice example of this in one of the earliest surviving plaques that decorate the inside of the Dome of the Rock. The plaque bears a celebratory inscription which honours the building of the Dome and the glory of its builder, Abdel Malik. Except that the name of Abdel Malik has been crudely painted over and replaced by the name of a caliph of a later generation whose family was bitterly opposed to the family of the Dome's actual builder. The revision is so poorly executed that the date has been left from the original inscription, even though the newly celebrated ruler wasn't even alive at that time! The internal politics of the Muslim rulers is literally written and rewritten on the walls of the Dome of the Rock.

The writing – and rewriting – of the history of the Temple and the Temple Mount is continuous, and often shows the allegiance of the author as clearly as the plaque in the Dome of the Rock. I began this book with Josephus' account of the destruction of the Temple. It was Josephus who wrote that Titus opposed the burning of the Temple – and even that he ran from his tent in a desperate attempt to save it. Josephus was a Jewish historian, but he wrote under the patronage of Titus himself, and he knew how to praise the Roman by celebrating his clemency, an exemplary virtue for an emperor to display. It's not by chance that the story of Titus' attempt to save the Temple of the Jews is written by a Jewish historian who is deeply beholden to the emperor about whom he is writing: the noble desire to save this sacred building speaks both to Jewish allegiances and to the ideals of Roman self-presentation. By contrast, Sulpicius Severus, a Christian historian of the fourth century, reveals a very different agenda. He declares that Titus overturned the advice of his generals, who actually wanted to save the Temple, and personally led his hesitant troops in the sack of the sanctuary. Titus' motivation, says Sulpicius Severus, was his desire to crush Christianity by attacking its Jewish roots. A Christian writing for Christian masters, Sulpicius Severus is keen to show that those emperors who did not adopt Christianity were the evil enemies of the newly successful religion. There is no stage in the history of the Temple – certainly none today – where we do not find such tendentious and conflicting accounts.

Yet for all the violence and political conflict, the Temple has also prompted the most beautiful poetry and art and the deepest of religious yearnings for a better world. The image of rebuilding the lost Temple – dreaming of Jerusalem, weeping for Zion – has proved one of the most powerful expressions of human desire to transcend the nasty and brutish particulars of this life. The visionary Romantic poet William Blake was typical in his profound attraction to the idea of a new and better world embodied in the Temple of Jerusalem. His searing distaste for contemporary society has been turned, with bitter irony, into a popular and pious hymn, but his words go to the heart of the history of the Temple:

> I will not cease from mental fight,
> Nor shall my Sword sleep in my hand,
> Till we have built Jerusalem
> In England's green and pleasant Land.

The desire to build anew demands 'mental fight': an act of the mind. The Temple, lost and reconstructed, yearned for and mourned for, pictured and sung about, is above all else a monument of the imagination.

....

2

SOLOMON'S TEMPLE: THE GLORY
AND THE DESTRUCTION

LAYING THE FOUNDATIONS: THE BOOK OF KINGS

The Temple of Solomon, the House of the Name of the Lord God, is the model for all the other temples, physical and imaginary, which are built over the centuries. This is the building that is usually and simply called the Temple. It emerges as the glorious central image of the two Books of Kings in the Bible, but even there it is already touched with the despair of its inevitable destruction. The Book of Kings was actually written *after* the Temple had been destroyed, and it looks back at the Temple's foundation with yearning for past majesty. The story of the Temple has to begin by looking at how the Book of Kings constructs this foundational image, and the place to start is with the figure who is the most richly characterised in the whole Bible, namely King David.

It's no surprise that the story of David is a favourite of modern novelists and artists from well before Michelangelo's famous statue to today: the combination of beautiful songs, political shenanigans and a wild sex life make him a natural hero for modernity. His life is told in remarkable depth, from the killing of Goliath as a boy, through his friendship with Jonathan and violent desire for Bathsheba, to his long and turbulent rule as king over the unified kingdom of Israel and Judah. The heroes of the Hebrew Bible are never perfect saints, but David combines extremes in a more complex and troubling way than anyone else. His political manipulations, sexual rapaciousness and family tragedies are recounted in stirring and disturbing detail, yet the Psalms transmitted in his name remain the basis of the liturgy for Jewish and Christian worship: he embodies the power of pious prayer as well as the achievements of the greatest of kings. It was David who made Jerusalem his capital after he had captured it from the Jebusites, the local tribe who had founded the city. It was also David who brought to Jerusalem the Ark of the Covenant, the holy cabinet which was the most sacred object of the Israelite religion. The Ark had been captured by the Philistines in war and, when returned, it had been temporarily housed in a shrine some eight miles from Jerusalem. David led the procession which escorted the Ark to his new capital, 'leaping and dancing before the Lord'.

The politics of this ceremonial seem clear enough. David had extended and strengthened the rule of his predecessor, Saul, over the united kingdoms of Israel in the north and Judah in the south. He had ruled for seven years from Hebron and now was moving to Jerusalem. The new administrative capital was to be the centre of religious life also. David, as the book of Samuel tells it, intended to complete this centralisation with a building programme: 'Here am I dwelling in a house of cedar, while the Ark of the Lord dwells in a tent!'. But the narrative then takes an unexpected turn. Nathan the prophet arrives and declares that this is not the will of God. When the Israelites were wandering in the desert, Nathan states, the Lord did not need a fixed house

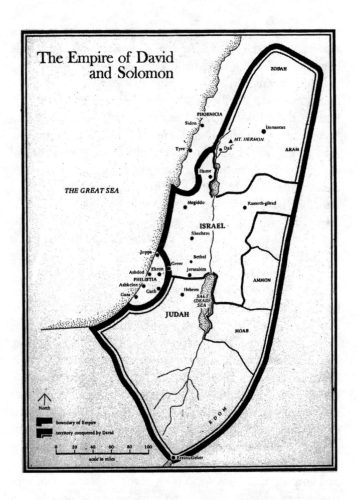

The Empire of David
and Solomon

ZOBAH

PHOENICIA
Sidon

Damascus

▲ MT. HERMON
Tyre
Dan

ARAM

Hazor

THE GREAT SEA

Megiddo

Ramoth-gilead

ISRAEL
Shechem

Joppa

Bethel

Gezer
Ashdod
Ekron
Jerusalem
PHILISTIA
Ashkelon
Gath

AMMON

Gaza

Hebron
SALT
(DEAD)
SEA

JUDAH

MOAB

EDOM

North

boundary of Empire

territory conquered by David

0   20   40   60   80   100
scale in miles

Ezion-Geber

5. A map of the territory of David's and Solomon's kingdom, marked by the heavy line. After Solomon's reign, the kingdom fell apart into smaller warring regions. The boundaries, marked in thinner lines, are very rough, and changed over the centuries.

[21]

(*bayit* – a temple) and so he does not need one now; but he *will* establish the house (*bayit* – a dynasty) of David, the dynasty from which the Messiah will come.

The blocking of David's desire to build the Temple is a telling moment. The Book of Chronicles, written a good deal later than the Book of Kings, is more sharply precise, stating that this bar is because David is not the right man for the job. He may choose the site for the Temple, draw up its plans and collect the funds to build it, but he is refused the honour of constructing so holy a sanctuary because he is a 'warrior and a man of blood'. His violence undermines his piety. But in the version we find in the Book of Kings, as so often in the Hebrew Bible, the play on words suggests that there is another question lurking here too. How should the building of the Temple (*bayit*) be related to the building of a dynasty (*bayit*)? The five books of Moses had no place for a king for the Israelites, but now we are entering a new period of Jewish history, where kings and dynasties indeed dominate the political landscape. The pun on *bayit* marks the necessary gap between the house of God and the house of a political ruler.

David draws up the plans, then, but Solomon, David's son and heir, the wisest of men, is the king chosen to complete the building of the Temple. It is to be a 'House for the Name of the Lord God'. This is a phrase worth pondering. In the ancient Mediterranean, from our earliest records to the Roman Empire and beyond, there were innumerable temples and holy shrines, from small piles of rocks on mountain tops to the Parthenon in Athens, and there were many similarities in ancient religions from region to region. Temples normally contained an image of the divinity (which was usually anthropomorphic, though certainly not always so), and sacrifices were offered to the god at the temple. Monumental temples were both expressions of a community's religion and a statement of the community's power and status. A temple was an easily recognisable feature of the Mediterranean landscape.

Solomon's building was a monumental temple for a national religion, but it was otherwise a very weird temple indeed. It was a temple not for God, but for God's *Name*. This explains how a house could be built for a god who is without bodily form and who is everywhere. It is a temple where the special presence of divinity can be perceived and acknowledged. But it is also a temple which has to observe the commandment of Exodus: 'Thou shalt make no graven image ... thou shalt not bow down to them or serve them'. This commandment has far-reaching theological and artistic implications, and certainly demands that there should be no image of God in the Temple. The Ark was to be kept in the Temple's deepest and holiest recesses, but already by the time of the destruction of Solomon's Temple even that had disappeared. It was buried, according to the rabbis, beneath the Temple Mount awaiting the Messiah, a story which was the basis for the Hollywood blockbuster *Raiders of the Lost Ark*. (The film, like the Book of Exodus, imagines the Ark is the focus for the power and presence of God; the Book of Deuteronomy, by contrast, says the Ark contained the stone tablets of the Law which Moses carried down from Mount Sinai.) It remained inexplicable and simply amazing to the later Greeks and Romans that there was *nothing to see* at the centre of the Jewish Temple. This was a house for an invisible, intangible and unrepresentable divinity. As conceived by the books of Kings and Chronicles, the Temple of Solomon

was a unique religious expression, formed in the twin cru-
cibles of biblical law and monumentalising zeal.

But the Temple was extraordinary in another way, too. It
became the centre of national religion in a wholly novel and
unparalleled manner. According to the Book of Kings, King
Hezekiah and then, most successfully, King Josiah demanded
the abolition of *all* cultic activity throughout the kingdom
outside Jerusalem, and a restriction of *all* religious service to
the Temple in Jerusalem. There were many religious sites in
Judah and Israel, shrines like Shiloh, where the Ark had been
kept for years, pillars where Jews worshipped and altars for
sacrifice. According to the Book of Kings, all of these were to
be destroyed, along with all vestiges of local cult – the most
familiar style of religion around the Mediterranean. All Jews
in Judah and Israel had to come to Jerusalem to worship,
especially on the three pilgrim festivals of Passover, Sukkot
(Tabernacles), and Shavuot (Pentecost).

Now, the Book of Kings was written many years after the
events it describes, and no doubt has its own retrospective
agenda. But that does not take away from the fact that the
ideal it promotes is unique. What is so bizarre about the
Temple is not the fact that the national, communal event of
religion had a central and most important site, but the fact
that the Temple became the *one and only* shrine for the whole
country. This is especially surprising at a period when travel
was dangerous and costly in time and effort, and when local
affiliations might be expected to be more pressing than a
national claim. Nor was this just a question of the celebration
of the major festivals. The religious ceremony of the sacrifice
of animals on an altar was a regular occasion on which the
community came together as a community in the worship of

God; it also produced meat for human consumption. In most of the Mediterranean, sacrifice was practised in innumerable local and even domestic settings. From now on, all sacrifice in Israel and Judah had to be held at only one place: the capital ruled over by David's dynasty. This was a staggering gesture of religious politics.

The institution of the Temple fully established the power of the priests, the *cohanim*, who officiated at the Temple and controlled the site, along with the *leviim* (Levites), who guarded the site and assisted the priests. (Both are inherited statuses, passed down through the father's line.) The post of High Priest remained a crucial political one throughout the history of ancient Israel. But above all, the Temple fundamentally changed the social structure of Israelite religious practice under the authority of the king. The Israelites become centred on the Temple of Jerusalem. From its very beginning, the Temple is tied up with national and religious politics.

BUILDING THE TEMPLE

The building of the Temple is described with lavish and intent detail in the Book of Kings. The narrative glorifies Solomon's international status and his power: its building is a product of treaties between countries, and the huge numbers of workers and the splendid materials involved are proudly itemised. Hiram, King of Tyre, agreed to provide cypress wood and cedar from Lebanon, as well as the required expertise in stone cutting; Solomon married the daughter of the Pharaoh of Egypt while building the Temple. Solomon imposed forced labour on 30,000 Israelites, who had to work in Lebanon on a three-month rota in shifts of 10,000 each month, cutting wood. He also had 70,000 porters and 80,000 quarriers for the stone, with 3,300 officials who supervised the work. Non-fundamentalists will feel no compulsion to believe these figures: they are there to express the immensity of the project.

It is something of a surprise, then, to modern ideas of grandeur that, despite the numbers of workers, the building itself was not massive. This first Temple was 60 cubits long, 20 cubits wide and 30 cubits high (though Chronicles says it was 120 cubits high, a figure which is taken by modern scholars to be impossible and a sign that the text is corrupt at that point). There was a 10-cubit deep vestibule or porch along the front, and a portico of side rooms along the other three sides. It may seem a trifle unhelpful of me to have given the measurements in cubits, the units which the Book of Kings uses, but one of the more vexing of scholarly arguments is exactly how long a cubit was. The different positioning of the Holy of Holies, say, can turn on just how long you think a cubit is, so this question of millimetres goes to the heart of the politics of reconstruction concerning the Temple. What fuels this debate is not just religious or archaeological nicety, but also claims of origin, ownership and authority – life and death matters. For those involved in these arguments 'accuracy' has become an ideologically charged issue which is debated with a ferocity that can seem out of all proportion. Almost every book on the Temple is obsessed with precise measurements, despite or because of the fact that there is no Temple to measure. So giving figures in cubits has a certain usefulness … But it will not be too misleading to say that the Temple was about 30 metres long, 10 metres wide and 15

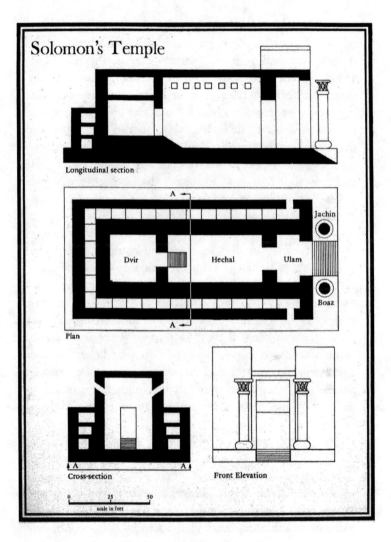

Solomon's Temple

Longitudinal section

A →

Jachin

Dvir   Hechal   Ulam

Boaz

A →

Plan

Cross-section

Front Elevation

A   A

0   25   50
scale in feet

6. A Plan of Solomon's Temple.

[27]

metres high. If you include the walls, porch and porticos, the outside measurements of the whole structure were about 50 metres long and 25 metres wide – that is, the size of an Olympic swimming pool or, for a more relevant comparison, about two-thirds of the size of the Parthenon. But the building was decorated to display all the magnificence of Solomon's wealth. The interior was panelled with cedar, and the entire building was overlaid with gold inside and out.

The ground-plan of the Temple was simple, rectangular and typical of religious sanctuaries that archaeologists have discovered in Canaan and Syria. Figure 6 shows one reconstruction which gives some sense the basic form, although, as ever when a text is used to reconstruct a building, there is plenty of room for disagreement and competing versions. (Figures 23, 24, 25 and 30 show the immense variety of possible reconstructions from the same text!) The vestibule or porch (*ulam*) led into a main sanctuary (*hechal*) and then to a Holy of Holies or inner sanctum (*dvir*): the worshipper's eyes were drawn up from the entrance towards the most sacred point. There were carved doors of olive wood overlaid with gold between the porch and the main sanctuary and between the main sanctuary and the Holy of Holies. Steps led up to the porch, and from the main sanctuary to the Holy of Holies.

Inside the Holy of Holies itself was the Ark of the Covenant, flanked by two huge statues of cherubim, 5 metres high with outstretched wings, made of olive wood covered with gold – these figures have particularly stimulated the imaginings of artists over the years. On either side of the entrance to the porch were placed two huge hollow bronze columns – nearly 12 metres high and 2 metres in diameter –

decorated with a motif of pomegranates and topped with lilies. They were cast by Hiram, a master builder sent by King Hiram of Tyre, and were called Jachin and Boaz – names which probably mean 'may he establish' and 'in strength', though there are many symbolic interpretations of what the pillars represent. They too have a long history in the Western imagination.

It was these columns which inspired the seventeenth-century Italian artist Bernini, for example, when he built the columns of the Baldacchino, the celebrated monument which rises above the tomb of St Peter in the centre of St Peter's at Rome – taking the symbolic architecture of the Temple into the heart of Catholic Christianity. The medieval presbytery, which the current St Peter's replaces, had been decorated with twelve twisted white marble columns which, the myth went, had been brought to Rome by Constantine from Solomon's Temple. Bernini's new design echoed the shape of these pillars, though Bernini's are bronze like the Temple's, and the angels that are sculpted around the top of the Baldacchino also recall the cherubim in the Temple.

Bernini was following a long-standing analogy. Tiberio Alferano, a cleric of St Peter's who died in 1596, wrote, 'The Emperor Constantine and Pope Sylvester did no differently about the body and the altar of the apostle Peter than Moses and Aaron had done about the Ark of the Covenant ... which at God's command they constructed in the centre of the Tabernacle under the wings of Cherubim. And Solomon did the same in the Temple.' As the tomb of St Peter is like the Ark, so the church is like the Temple – and draws on its symbolic weight. The analogy is emphasised in the building's decorations. If you stand in the Chapel of the Holy

Sepulchre in St Peter's and look up at the ceiling, you will see there a stucco relief of Solomon building the Temple. The columns look exactly like those of the Baldacchino.

Around the Temple was a large stone-walled courtyard where the people gathered for religious ceremonies and for the sacrifices in particular. In this courtyard, there was an altar of bronze, 10 metres square, with tables for the bread and other offerings, also in bronze. There was a huge bowl of bronze, over 5 metres in diameter, resting on twelve bronze oxen, which held perhaps 70,000 litres of water and was called 'the sea'. Around it were ten bronze stands for ritual washing, each elaborately carved and wheeled.

On the same site Solomon also built two palaces: his own, the Lebanon Forest House, and a smaller palace for his wife, the Pharaoh's daughter, whom he had married to cement diplomatic relations with the great kingdom of Egypt. These are buildings flamboyantly designed to express the glory of the king. The palace of Solomon was four times the size of the Temple (100 cubits long, 50 cubits wide, and 30 cubits high), held up by three rows of fifteen columns each; it was panelled in cedar, with three tiers of square windows, and was divided into a portico where Solomon sat in judgement, and a rear courtyard where his residential palace was. The close link between the royal dynasty and the worship of the Lord was powerfully instantiated in the linked building complex of Temple and palace. The political authority of Solomon sat side by side with the religious law of God. As in so many ancient Middle Eastern kingdoms, the king, as shepherd of the people, provided a mediation between the people and divinity.

So far, I have been describing the building of the Temple as it is represented in the Book of Kings. The only evidence for the first Temple is scriptural – this written text from the Bible: there are no accounts from outsiders and no material remains. The Bible offers a glorious picture of the wisest of men, Solomon, following God's commands in building a magnificent house for worship. The ground-plan of the Temple clearly echoes the description of the Tabernacle and camp of the Israelites wandering in the desert on their way to the Promised Land as portrayed in the Book of Exodus. Each night the Ark of the Covenant was placed in the Tabernacle and the Israelites formed a rectangular camp around it; in the same way the Holy of Holies is set in the sanctuary of the Temple and surrounded by the people of Israel in the courtyard. The Temple is, as it were, the civic equivalent of the nomadic Tabernacle, and so the sacrificial laws laid down in scripture form the basis of the rituals of the Temple. Exodus is written as if it were the unfolding historical narrative of the Jews' struggle to become a people and to reach the Promised Land. The Book of Kings celebrates the establishment of David's and Solomon's kingdom in the Promised Land. In all the Hebrew Bible there is only one event that is dated by reference to the Exodus, and that is the building of the Temple: its foundations were laid 'in the four hundred and eightieth year after the Israelites left the land of Egypt'. The Book of Kings is in this way written as if the Temple were the fulfilment of the promise of Exodus – and so it has been read by the pious over many generations.

Things are not so straightforward, however. First, scholars who study the Bible from a historical perspective put a lot of weight on the fact that the Book of Kings was finished after the destruction of the Temple, with which it ends. That is, it is written, according to the book's own chronology, at least 400 years after the foundation it purports to describe. Even if it contains material that stretches back to the times it portrays, it has certainly been edited – rewritten – from a new perspective. Like all military, religious and political history, it has an agenda. Solomon was already a legendary figure of a golden age, when the kingdom of the Israelites was united and internationally powerful, and when religion flourished, quite unlike the weakened, impoverished and fragmented Jewish people of the later period, always under the power of one empire or another. This glorious Temple was already an object of ancient nostalgia. After all, even when the Temple was destroyed, its most holy sacred object, the Ark of the Covenant, had long since disappeared. The Book of Kings is to be read as full of the desire, fantasies and hopes of a nationalist author looking back to a lost age of glory, majesty and closeness to God. A building of gold – a show of power, wealth and international position, a sign of God's establishment of a glorious dynasty – speaks to many needs.

Indeed, since the nineteenth century, theologians have been keen to find different agendas or political strands in the biblical texts, and thus to find the different historical layers of the composition of the text. Some of the Psalms refer directly to the Babylonian exile, and so where the pious have continued to see David as a divinely inspired prophet of an event centuries in the future, critical scholars have preferred to see the Psalms as a collection of songs written and put together over many generations, and ascribed to David by tradition. Even the passages in Exodus about the Tabernacle are seen by some modern scholars as a late addition to the biblical text, a retrospective justification for the form of the Temple. For today's critical theologians the narrative of the foundation of the Temple in the Book of Kings is not the fulfilment of the promise of Exodus, but a politically and religiously partial account, marked by its historical composition among post-exilic Jews.

THE YARDSTICK OF IDEALISM

The destruction of the Temple is a defining moment of Jewish history towards which the narrative of the Book of Kings leads, and which the Books of Jeremiah and Lamentations in particular mourn with their stirring outbursts of profound grief, desperate confusion and anger. The Temple indeed looms over the whole history narrated in the Book of Kings. After the death of Solomon, the united kingdom broke down into repeated conflict between the states of Israel and Judah, each with its own king, and into repeated wars with neighbouring states (Figure 5 shows the rough and much-contested boundary lines). It's not a part of the Bible that is foremost in most people's reading these days. Each king's reign, however, is introduced with a summary of his behaviour with regard to the established religion of the Temple. So Ahab, who reigned over Israel for twenty-two years, is announced with: 'Ahab son of Omri did what was displeasing to the Lord, more than all who preceded him. Not content to follow the sins of Jeroboam son of Nebat, he took to wife Jezebel daughter of King Ethbaal of the Phoenicians, and he went and served Baal and worshipped him. He erected an altar to Baal ... Ahab also made a sacred post.' The phrase 'did what was displeasing to the Lord', or 'did evil in the eyes of the Lord' as the Authorised Version has it, is a formula that introduces each bad king, just as 'did what is pleasing to the Lord' is applied to each good king. But there is also a more nuanced map of iniquity. So Hoshea 'did what was displeasing to the Lord, but not as much as the kings of Israel who preceded him'; and even a good king such as Joash, who restored Temple cult, falls short because 'the shrines were not removed; the people continued to sacrifice and make offerings at the shrines'. A king's reign is defined according to whether he followed the ancestral religion of the Temple and maintained the Temple as the sole place of sacrifice – a pattern which powerfully expresses the religious agenda of the author. Throughout the generations there is a constant battle over the continuation of shrines, posts and sacrifices outside Jerusalem, and between the worship of the God of the Israelites and competing local religions. It is a history which reveals just how bold and impossible an idea it proved to demand a centralised cult and single Temple of the Name of God.

Solomon's ideal, however, is the yardstick of judgement for all the kings, just as his own failure to live up to it provides the model for each subsequent ruler. The history of the Book of Kings is framed by the Temple: the foundation of the Temple dominates the opening chapters, ends with its destruction, and in between tells a narrative of constant conflict between the ideal model of Temple worship and the threat of idolatry, civil strife and moral transgression. What has made the first Temple so powerful an image is this intense combination of glorious idealism constantly haunted from the very beginning by man's inability to live up to it.

BUILDING A SCAFFOLD ROUND THE TEMPLE: THE STORIES OF THE MIDRASH

There is another set of ancient stories, known as the *Midrash*, which develop with wonderful expressiveness these two aspects of the Temple – an image of a lost golden age and the recognition that it is destined for destruction. The *Midrash* is a type of commentary on scriptural texts, most often in the form of short narratives which explain and expand upon the bare biblical narrative. They are collected in their own books of compilation and also rehearsed in the Talmud; they are stories with a moral point and with a certain authority (although they cannot be used to make religious law), and they are also often funny, poignant or full of the weird extravagances of myth and folklore. There are hundreds of such brief tales, especially from the first six centuries AD, which give an extraordinary insight into how the establishment of the Temple was being constantly thought about and understood in fresh ways. The *Midrash* surrounds the edifice of the Books of Kings with a scaffold of annotation. The memory of the Temple was explored, buttressed and passed on through the constant telling of such stories. Through them, we can see the idea of the Temple under construction.

The tales certainly dwell lovingly on the fabulous nature of the Temple.

There was a kind of worm/reptile called a shamir *which was made at twilight on the sixth day of creation, together with other extraordinary things. It was about as large as a barley corn, and it possessed the remarkable property of cutting the hardest of diamonds. The* shamir *was used for hewing into shape the stones from which the Temple was built, because the law prohibited iron tools to be used for the work on the Temple. The* shamir *was guarded in Paradise until Solomon needed it. He sent an eagle to fetch the worm. With the destruction of the Temple, the* shamir *vanished.*

Now, the narrative of the Book of Kings has this sentence: 'no hammer or axe or any iron tool was heard in the House as it was being built'. At one level, it prompts a judgement from religious authorities, which prohibits iron from being used in building the Temple. But it also prompts the *Midrash*'s story of a lost age of miraculous creatures from Paradise. With the *shamir* the builders did not need iron. The Temple was so marvellous that it could not have been constructed by human hands alone. In the same spirit, we are told how a genie from a bottle brought up the foundation stone from the bottom of the Red Sea. Other miracles are more mundane, though, for anyone who has had building work done, none the less miraculous: not one worker fell ill during the whole period of the building; the expected forty days of rain, which fell every year, stopped in order to allow the construction work to be finished smoothly and on schedule.

A particularly touching story explains the choice of the site for the Temple not as part of the power play of David's regime, nor as the spot where Abraham bound Isaac, but rather as motivated by a homely ethical lesson:

A heavenly voice directed Solomon to go to Mount Zion at night, to a field owned jointly by two brothers. One of the brothers was a bachelor and poor, the other was blessed both with wealth and a large family of children. It was harvesting time. Under cover of night, the poor brother kept adding to the other's heap of grain, for, although he was poor, he thought his brother needed more on account of his large family. The rich brother, in the same clandestine way, added to the poor brother's store, thinking that though he had a family to support, the other was without means. This field, Solomon concluded, which had called forth so remarkable a manifestation of brotherly love, was the best site for the Temple and he bought it.

This story takes on its full symbolic weight when juxtaposed with all the murderous founding brothers of the Bible from Cain and Abel onwards (not to mention the subsequent history of violence over the Temple Mount between the descendants of Abraham). In typical folkloric style, the *Midrash* makes the foundational moment of national religious cult a family story of caring, a story of values from which anyone can learn.

It's more surprising and less comfortable to find bitter little tales that re-read the foundation story in the light of the destruction to come. In the Book of Kings itself, the end of Solomon's life is shocking, and all too often ignored. The wisest of men, says Kings, loved and married many foreign women – despite the fact that such unions were banned by the religious law. These women led Solomon astray towards other religions, and in his old age he 'did what was displeasing to the Lord and did not remain loyal to the Lord like his father David'. Not only did he follow the divinities of the Phoenicians and the Ammonites, he even built shrines for them on the hills around Jerusalem. For Kings, this sin explains why the unified kingdom of Solomon did not last, and we will see shortly how this narrative pattern becomes a dominant model for writing the history of the kings of

Israel and Judah. But the *midrashim* take this story of the heretical Solomon, the wise man turned bad, and spin it out in fascinating ways.

Solomon, one story goes, married Pharaoh's daughter on the self-same day as the consecration of the Temple, and the rejoicing for the wedding was even more lavish than the rejoicing for the Temple. That's why, says the *Midrash*, Isaiah declares, 'This city hath been to me a provocation of mine anger and my fury from the day that they built it even unto this day'. The *Midrash* typically reads a biblical text with an intense focus and develops stories to explain every narrative detail, including the silences. Since the Lord says that his anger and fury are provoked 'from the day that they built it' there must have been something that happened on the day of the Temple's building that enraged God. So we get this story: Pharaoh's daughter 'spread over Solomon's bed a canopy studded with diamonds and pearls, which gleamed and glittered like the constellations in the sky'. Consequently, Solomon thought it was still night whenever he woke up. So he slept late and the morning sacrifice was missed on the very day of the Temple's dedication, because 'the keys of the Temple lay under his pillow and none dared wake him'. Bathsheba, his mother, who knew a good deal about wifely persuasion, was outraged. Everyone will blame her as his mother, she complains, and she draws the moral 'Give not your strength unto women nor thy ways to them that destroy kings'. In the poignant retrospective story of the *Midrash*, from the very moment of its consecration the Temple was already destined to fall because it was sullied by Solomon's seduction by foreign women and other religions, and by disregard for his role as shepherd of the people.

Looking back, these Jewish authors imaginatively reconstructed the narrative of the foundation of the Temple to try to make sense of its history, and of the role of the image of the Temple in their thinking. This creative building of story upon story about the Temple continues throughout the centuries – and it still continues to make up our image of the Temple.

The shocking and total destruction of the Temple of the omnipotent God by the Babylonian king Nebuchadnezzar cried out for explanation. How could God have allowed his house to be so ravaged? The Book of Kings offers a grand narrative of royal misdeeds as explanation. The wrath of God could not be assuaged even by the best of the kings, Josiah, who did reinstitute proper Temple worship and who also destroyed all the shrines outside the Temple. But the work of explanation continued to flower and was far more varied than that offered by the narrative of Kings. The *Midrash Eicha Rabbah* is a collection of *midrashim* on the Book of Lamentations. It begins with thirty-four chapters of 'proems', introductory paragraphs for sermons on the subject of the destruction of the Temple: obviously rabbis then as now needed help in explaining to the people how awful and total destruction could have happened to the godly. These proems are followed with an immense collection of explanatory paraphrases, homiletic stories and religious discussion of every phrase of Lamentations, the most haunting poetry of mourning for the loss of the Temple. These show a quite different version of why the Temple fell. Here is a passage from the second chapter of proems, which uses an imagined dialogue of the enemy to get its point across:

The pagan philosophers were asked 'Can we overcome this people of Israel?' They replied, 'Go round to their synagogues; if there is a hum of children's voices studying Torah [biblical scripture], you cannot prevail over them.'

The Temple was sacked because there wasn't enough intellectual study in the synagogues! This tale reflects a different and much later world than the time of Solomon or the prophets. There are no synagogues or rabbis mentioned in the Book of Kings or Samuel; but for this story the synagogues, houses for prayer, where sacrifice is not practised, are what really count. Education and study have become the privileged expressions of a pious life. What determines the people's fate is not the behaviour of powerful rulers but how children learn. This is the world where rabbis, not priests, are dominant; where the honoured place is not the Temple court but the schoolroom. Rabbi Simeon ben Yochai taught: 'If you behold cities uprooted from their site in the land of Israel, know that the inhabitants failed to pay the teachers of Bible.' It's amusing to see the self-interest of the religious authority here – proper pay for teachers is always an issue – but it should not obscure the shift of perspective. With the loss of the Temple and its ritual, study of the law becomes a prime activity of the religious: one scholar explained why he remained in Babylon even after the exile was over on the grounds that 'the study of the Law is more important than the building of the Temple'. It is in such a context that the fall of the Temple can be explained as the lack of proper studying in the community. Each explanation of why the Temple was destroyed is always also a way of talking about the writer's own preoccupations and own understanding of society and its relation to God.

The Temple can never be described merely in architectural terms. It is imaged – made up – in a swirl of stories. Its description is always part of writing history. The Temple is not just a building, but a way of expressing the hopes of religious idealism, and of constructing a picture of humanity's relation to the divine. From the Book of Kings onwards, writing about Solomon's Temple means imagining a building which no longer has any physical existence, and that is one reason why its construction and destruction have become such potent imaginative symbols for the aspirations and failings of humanity.

3

···

REBUILDING THE TEMPLE:
A VISION FROM EXILE

'LET THEM MEASURE THE PATTERN'

The destruction of the Temple leads to an inevitable desire
for rebuilding: the search for foundations. A second Temple
was constructed in Jerusalem after the Jews' return from exile
in Babylon, but the idea of a return to Zion to build a new
house of God motivated visionaries, prophets and exiles alike
to create their own images of a future Temple. Across the
centuries, 'rebuilding the Temple' has remained an inspira-
tional clarion call for a spiritual idealism more even than for
a real building. Every such call for rebuilding echoes the biblical books of the prophets, those most powerful expressions
of grief, hope and the demand for spiritual and political
change.

All the great prophets whose books are set at the end of
the first-Temple period in the sixth century BC are represented as men fully engaged in the political turmoil of their
own times, and each is obsessed with loss, lamentation and
the consolation of reconstruction. Jeremiah, for example,
captures with stark vividness the emotional traumas that the
destruction caused. He foretold the loss of the Temple, but
his prophecies were so strident and depressing that he was

actually banned from its precincts. (The word 'jeremiad' for a powerful speech of woe and lamentation has its root here.) He was so sure of future consolation, however, that when Nebuchadnezzar did attack, he advised offering no resistance: he walked round with a yoke on his neck to symbolise his submission, a gesture which did not endear him to the besieged and fighting Israelites. After the capture of Jerusalem he too was led to exile in Egypt, from where he advised the Israelites to settle down in Babylon because he also predicted a return after seventy years.

This strange mixture of alienation and hope, passivity and passion, destruction and consolation forms a powerful and disturbing message, but it is the idealist visions of the prophet Ezekiel above all which have inspired the passion for rebuilding the Temple. Ezekiel was a priest who was exiled to Babylon, where he was inspired to deliver the judgements and prophecies which make up the Book of Ezekiel. Central to this book too is an image of the Temple.

Ezekiel begins, 'In the thirtieth year on the fifth day of the fourth month, when I was in the community of exiles by the Chebar Canal, the heavens opened and I saw a vision of God', and his dark and disturbing visions from exile have had a profound impact on Western artists from Raphael to Hieronymus Bosch to William Blake, none more so than his intensely powerful and strange vision of the Temple to come and God enthroned within it. Here, Ezekiel is led by a man whose 'appearance was like bronze, with a line of flax and a measuring rod in his hand'. This guide proceeds to give lengthy and detailed measurements and a design for a Temple similar to those of Solomon's. But God himself appears 'from the east with a roar like the roar of mighty

[43]

waves', and his voice is heard promising to dwell in the Temple for ever. The message is encapsulated in these memorable words:

> *Thou son of Man, shew the house to the house of Israel, that they may be ashamed of their iniquities: and let them measure the pattern.*

The Temple of Ezekiel's vision is of a heavenly design, which is to be a lesson in morality to the house of Israel. They are to 'measure the pattern' – and measure up to the law. It is the projection of an ideal religious space, where a noble ruler and holy caste of priests worship the present God, where sacred and profane, pure and impure are carefully distinguished and where the order of things is established, fixed and true.

This image from exile became a dominant model for Christian ideals of the celestial Temple and, following God's command to measure the pattern, architectural visionaries in medieval and Renaissance Europe constructed model after model of Ezekiel's Temple. Figure 7 shows the plan and elevation of the entrance to Ezekiel's Temple precinct from a woodcut of Anton Koberger's 1481 edition of the influential Bible commentary of Nicolaus de Lyra, known as the *Postillae*. It shows clearly enough how the image of the distant Holy Land is constructed out of the materials of medieval northern Europe. (The bolts on the door are particularly telling.) Figure 8, a print by Matthias Hafenreffer from 150 years later, reconstructs the whole Temple precinct, carefully ordered like so many Renaissance drawings of cities or military camps. Both artists were pious and scholarly men,

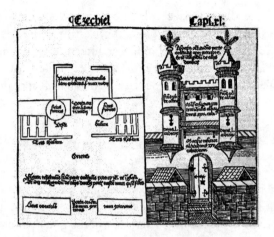

7. Ezechiel's Temple as imagined by Anton Koberger in 1481.

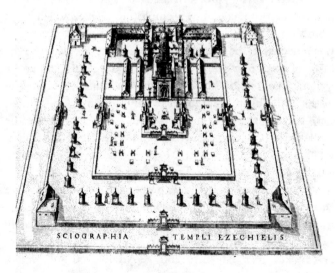

SCIOGRAPHIA TEMPLI EZECHIELIS.

8. Ezechiel's Temple as imagined by Matthias Hafenreffer in 1613.

[45]

but the two images have little in common. As with so many of the illustrations in this book, they testify to the power of the *idea* of the Temple: through architecture there emerges again and again an image of an ideal order. Far from Jerusalem, these artists could only dream of and draw a Temple to come.

'HOW DOES IT LOOK TO YOU NOW?'

The return from exile and the rebuilding of the Temple were rather more shabby and piecemeal than Ezekiel's vision, at any rate as it is told in the Books of Ezra and Nehemiah. The authority for the reconstruction had some grandeur at least. Cyrus the Great, founder of the Persian Empire, after he had conquered Babylon, provided the charter for Jews to go back to Jerusalem and rebuild the Temple. He even provided funds from the royal treasury for the project. The glory of the king was reflected in the happiness of his subject people, or so the myth of empire insists. Some Israelites did return, under the leadership of one Sheshbazzar. They built an altar at the site of the Temple, but the project faded into a mess of difficulties. In Darius' reign, more Israelites returned under the guidance of Zerubbabel and the High Priest Joshua (though, as before, many stayed in Mesopotamia in what became long-lived communities). The feast of Sukkot (Tabernacles) was once again celebrated at its proper site. Foundations were laid and work started; Zerubbabel started to bring cedars from Lebanon, as had Solomon. But almost immediately trouble broke out again. The Samaritans, who were descended from Israelites and Assyrians and followed a version of Israelite religion, wished to be involved in the construction; Zerubbabel refused. The row developed to such a degree that a royal decree was issued to stop the building. The bickering went on for years until a further royal decree was issued by Darius which allowed the second Temple to be finished in 515 BC.

The ground-plan and design, it is claimed, were the same as those of the Temple of Solomon. But there is little chance that the impoverished and few Jews of Jerusalem, in what was a backwater of empire, could have been able to reproduce the huge amounts of gold, wood and bronze or possessed the technical skills so celebrated in the Book of Kings. Moreover, a temple constructed following a written text or a childhood memory (at least seventy years separated the exile and the rebuilding) had little chance of being a precise reproduction. As the pictures in this book show, the building is repeatedly and differently reimagined from the same words. Most tellingly, the Book of Haggai, although he has high hopes for future glory, gives a rather depressing account of the foundation: 'Who is there left among you who saw this House in its former splendour? How does it look to you now? It must seem like nothing to you.' Even to one of God's prophets, the second Temple was not an impressive sight.

Nor is there any archaeological or historical evidence to suggest that Jerusalem was much more than an ignored backwater for the next two centuries, which saw Greek culture spreading through the Mediterranean. The city walls were rebuilt in the fifth century BC, according to the testy account of Nehemiah, another book of the bible; at the same time, King Artaxerxes allowed Ezra to return and establish the Torah of Moses as the official and authoritative law of the Jews. (There is little sign that the Jews had such a systematic legal code before.) Both Nehemiah and Ezra were closely associated with the Persian king's court, and since Jerusalem was still part of the Persian Empire, this insider politics was necessary for their mission. It is an irony of history that Judaism and the Temple were re-established in Jerusalem only thanks to the patronage of the Persian Empire – the territory of modern Iraq and Iran.

From the fourth to the second century BC the population of Jews grew in Judaea and, above all, the ideological pillars of the one God, the one Torah and the one Temple became defining elements of their cultural and national identity. This was a crucial period in the development of the Jewish community centred on the Temple, and of the community's self-perception as Jewish. There can be little doubt that the Temple and its staff of priests (*cohanim*) and attendants (*leviim*) enjoyed tremendous prestige among the general inhabitants of Judaea, that the Temple was central to the financial, religious and social fabric of the community, and that the authority of the religious law of the Torah played a major role both in the everyday lives of the inhabitants of Judaea and especially in the milieu of the educated elite. This is the fundamental background to the revolt of the Maccabees, which brings the second Temple into modern Jewish religious celebration with the festival of Chanukah, a memorial of the rededication of the Temple in the face of Greek cultural imperialism.

CELEBRATING THE CULTURAL REVOLUTION

This story begins with Alexander the Great, who conquered a huge area of the world from Greece to Iran to the borders of India, including ancient Palestine. In the wake of his armies and his zeal for founding new cities for his soldiers, Greek culture came to be the dominant value of social life across his huge conquered territories. Greek was the administrative language and the language of high culture; the gymnasium, theatre and symposia – formal drinking parties – were found everywhere, reaching as far as Afghanistan. Greek thought, especially a proper education in literature and philosophy, defined sophistication and cultivation. Its influence was pervasive, even in the Talmud, which tried hard to turn its back on the values of Hellenism. The *Midrash* often shows the Jews triumphing over their adversaries. Alexander the Great was said to have come to Jerusalem at the head of his conquering army. According to the *Midrash*, the High Priest, dressed in his formal regalia, went out to meet him on the road. Alexander, to everyone's astonishment, fell prostrate before the old man. Before his defeat of the Persians, Alexander had dreamt a prophecy that he would be victorious: the prophet had been exactly this figure of the High Priest. The fact that Alexander never visited Jerusalem at all helps us see this fiction for what it is – and the tensions that underlie such a story.

After Alexander's death, his kingdom was divided into more than one empire. Palestine, as ever, was fought over. It came under the control first of the Ptolemies of Egypt and then the Seleucids, and the rule of the Antiochus family, centred on Antioch in Syria. It was Antiochus IV in 168–167 BC who precipitated the Maccabean revolt. Antiochus tried to enforce a law banning the observance of Torah law, and he rededicated the Temple to Zeus Olympios–Baal Shamem. The reasons behind such aggressive cultural imperialism after many years of interaction between the Jewish and Greek communities are quite unclear, but the response – the Maccabean revolt – was severe and had long-lasting implications. The revolt was the work of a committed minority rather than any spontaneous mass uprising, but it gradually grew and coalesced under the leadership of the Hasmonean family and the charismatic Judah Maccabee. Initially, military opposition to the Seleucids was disastrous (Judah was killed and his army crushed in 161 BC). But eventually constant fighting over the throne back in Syria weakened the Seleucid Empire, and the revolt successfully allowed the establishment of a Hasmonean dynasty over Palestine.

Like all revolutions, the Maccabean revolt is surrounded with retrospective heroic and miraculous stories – which centre on the Temple. The most famous story became the basis for modern-day religious practice. When the Jewish forces retook the Temple from the Seleucids, they found it desecrated, and there was only one bottle left of the sacred oil which kept the seven-branch candelabrum permanently burning, as the law demanded. This was enough for one day only, but the nearest oil was eight days' transport away. They immediately sent for the oil but, miraculously, the single day's oil burnt for all eight days, and the light (of the Temple, of the revolution, of piety) was never extinguished. The rededication of the Temple was a new start for the Jewish kingdom.

This story is not included in the Book of Maccabees (the official history, as it were), but comes from a later rabbinical source; none the less it is the charter for the festival of Chanukah, still celebrated by Jews around the world. Chanukah means 'dedication', and it celebrates this rededication of the second Temple by lighting candles for eight days.

Because Chanukah is close to Christmas, and because the menorah, the candelabrum, is such a familiar symbol, it has become one of the most visible and recognisable of Jewish rituals (for all that it is not biblical in origin and, as festivals go, of secondary importance). In the multicultural world of English primary schools, it is often called a festival of light and equated with the Hindu and Sikh festival of Diwali and the recently concocted Christian ceremony for children called Christingle. What Chanukah memorialises, however, is the refoundation of the rebuilt Temple. It looks back to a time when the violent clash of cultures and communities offered the opportunity for the zealous defence and reconstruction of a religious ideal. Perhaps that is one reason why the festival has become increasingly visible in the modern exile of the Jewish communities of the diaspora.

A TEMPLE FOR PURISTS

The growth of a stronger sense of Jewish identity focused on the Temple also brought with it the growth of different sects of Judaism, the Pharisees and Sadducees in particular. Any system of law, especially one as complex and all-embracing as the Torah, results in negotiation, dissent and transgression as well as commitment from a populace, and any centralised religious authority can expect the complexities of shifting power relations to produce social divisiveness. The twentieth-century discovery of the Dead Sea Scrolls revitalised interest in one of these groups in particular, the Essenes. The Essenes were an extreme separatist group dedicated to purity: they observed the biblical laws of purity with maximum obsessiveness. This involved sometimes astounding rules of self-deprivation, and not just with regard to kosher food or to sex. For example, the Essenes were required to go a statutory distance outside the boundaries of their camp to defecate. Since nothing could be carried on the Sabbath, nor a trip of even quite a short length be undertaken, no defecation was allowed on the day of rest! (They were an attractive group to the early Christians, for whom self-deprivation was also a fascination.) The Essenes too, however, harboured a vision of rebuilding the Temple.

It was probably an Essene group which formed the settlement at Qumran as a deliberate retreat from the Temple in Jerusalem – they called themselves 'The Exiles in the Desert' – and it was in a cave in Qumran that one of the most remarkable of modern archaeological discoveries was made, the Temple Scroll. This long scroll – at more than 8 metres in length it is the longest of the Dead Sea Scrolls – written in a beautifully clear hand, describes a Temple and cult rules for a new, pure group of Jews. As another of the Qumran scrolls, the so-called Community Rule of the group, puts it, 'It shall be a House of Perfection and Truth in Israel'. This image of the Temple is based on Ezekiel (and also on Solomon's Temple) but has its own pattern of concentric rectangular construction, harking back to the Tabernacle in the desert. It is a temple of the future, and wonderfully captures the marginal sect's wish to fulfil its own dream of grandeur: 'If he walks in My statutes and observes My commandments and does what is right and good in my sight, a man of his sons shall not be cut off from sitting on the throne of the kingdom of Israel for ever.' Even while the Temple was still standing there were Jewish groups enthusiastically dreaming of rebuilding a new and

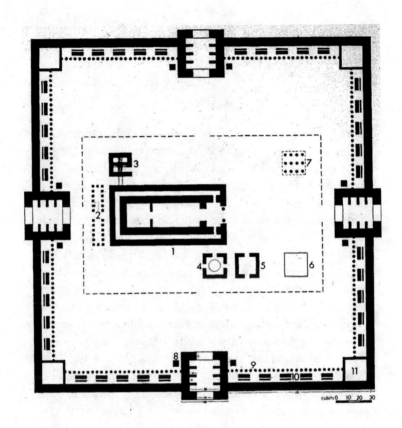

9. The Temple Scroll describes a future, new Temple for the Essenes of Qumran. Here is a plan of that building, drawn to scale according to the injunctions in the Temple scroll: (1) the Temple; (2) the Stoa of Columns; (3) the Stairhouse; (4) the House of the Laver; (5) the House of Utensils; (6) the Altar; (7) the slaughter-place (the 'Ceiling over the Twelve Pillars'); (8) the 'cooking places'; (9) the inner court Stoa; (10) the sitting places and tables; (11) the 'places for the stoves' – as imagined by the Israeli politician and archaeologist Yigael Yadin.

[53]

purer one. Whenever the Temple seemed corrupt, there were those who hoped, like the Book of 1 Enoch, for 'a new house, greater and loftier'.

LOOKING FOR MR X

Even the story of the scroll's recovery brilliantly illumines the longing that runs through the hope of rebuilding the Temple. Like most of the Dead Sea Scrolls, the Temple Scroll was found by chance by Bedouins – but fell into the hands of an unscrupulous dealer, Mr X. He allowed only tiny scraps that had fallen off the scroll to be seen, and tried to sell the whole mysterious manuscript secretly for a huge sum. The leading Israel archaeologist and future politician Yigael Yadin, whose father had been instrumental in recovering the first Dead Sea Scrolls to be found, was desperate to retrieve it: he negotiated repeatedly and unsuccessfully (and across several countries) with the dealer through an intermediary, Mr Z. After several years, all he knew was the dealer's name. In the 1967 war, Yadin was a leading military adviser, acting as the chief liaison officer between the prime minister and the minister of defence, Moshe Dayan. At the height of the battle for Jerusalem, he recalled that the dealer had a house in the Arab section of the city – until now unapproachable. After discussion with the prime minister and Moshe Dayan, he briefed a lieutenant-colonel of the Intelligence Corps with a description of the scroll and the address. The scroll was duly delivered by the taciturn officer during an intense meeting of the war cabinet discussing the attack on Syria. The scroll had been found under the floor tiles, damply rotting in a shoe-box, along with further scraps in a cigar box. The scroll now

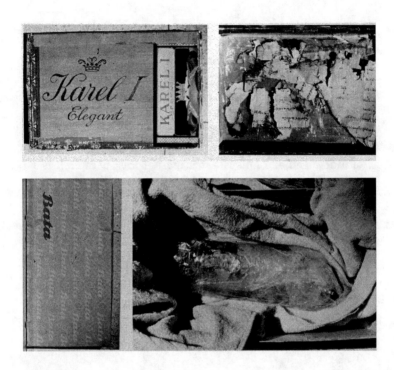

10. The Temple Scroll was discovered in a shoe-box, with fragments in a cigar box. Yigael Yadin, with the archaeologist's love of real, physical evidence gives us pictures of the two boxes.

has pride of place in the Israel Museum. The shoebox and the cigar box are both carefully illustrated in Yadin's wonderfully dramatic account of his search.

In the course of the battle for Jerusalem, which brought the Temple Mount once again under the authority of a Jewish state, an officer is directed by the very highest authorities to save a cultural treasure which seems especially precious, namely, an ancient, marginal and extreme sect's dream of a new Temple. This is a treasure not least because it is a sign and symbol of that time when the second Temple stood, itself so important to the different claims of legitimacy in the Middle East, claims being violently contested in the war itself. What is most striking about Yadin's story is the sheer complexity of how history, fantasy and the politics of yearning intertwine over the ages, and make the portrait of one man's search so intriguing a mix of the political and the personal. Such is the strange power of the idea of rebuilding the Temple.

4

HEROD'S TEMPLE:
A WONDER OF THE WORLD

A SPACE TO AMAZE THE SENSES

Herod's act of rebuilding the Temple is so grandiose and so successful that it makes even the Essenes' visionary dreams of a future Temple seem mealy-mouthed. He came to power in 37 BC and ruled until his death in 4 BC. He rose to his supreme position as a young commander who knew exactly how to exploit the political situation of petty warring between local rulers and the Roman Empire's government. He made alliances with both Jewish and pagan grandees across the region, and in particular befriended Mark Antony, Julius Caesar's right-hand man. It was thanks to Roman patronage that he became king over the Jews, and he administered the province for the Romans and his own benefit. The population and wealth of the Jewish community had greatly increased under the Hasmonean dynasty and this provided the financial basis for his grand projects. But there was a political agenda too. He rebuilt the harbour of Caesarea according to the latest architectural principles, fortified the kingdom's borders and reorganised its institutions to centralise his own power. He crippled the role of the traditional court of the Sanhedrin and restricted the position of High

Priest of the Temple, which used to last for life and had been passed down from father to son (a system that might have created a rival power base): from now on, the High Priest was appointed for an irregular period, and appointed exclusively by the king himself. Herod no doubt intended to create a strong, unified and lasting kingdom, with himself as uncontested ruler, and central to this was the rebuilding of Jerusalem and, above all, the Temple.

He reconstructed all the public spaces of the city and designed the Temple to be one of the very largest buildings in the Roman Empire, big enough to contain the vast numbers of pilgrims from his new kingdom (and beyond). Historians from the ancient world bitterly anatomise the nastiness of Herod's personality, and record the lurid family politics and violence of his reign. And lurid and nasty it was, with enough jealousies, sexual misdemeanours, poisonings, plots and double-crossings to create for the historians a perfect image of the decadence of the East combined with the corruption of empire. But Herod did change the status of Jerusalem. It was only after his policies of reconstruction that the Roman scholar Pliny the Elder could describe Jerusalem as 'by far the most famous city of the East'. And the Temple he built was a truly remarkable construction.

Josephus, the Jewish historian who wrote the most detailed account of the war which destroyed the Temple in AD 70, also gives us the most detailed account of its construction. Herod's motivation, he declares, was to make a building 'great enough to assure his eternal remembrance'; but the king also knew that it would be hard to persuade the people to allow the destruction of the long-honoured Temple of Zerubbabel. So he began his campaign of persuasion with a full-scale public speech. Like all good politicians, he reminded the Jews that they had never had it so good – 'I have by the will of God brought the Jewish nation to such a state of prosperity as it has never known before' – and he recalled the success of his current building programme. But the crucial argument was that Zerubbabel's Temple fell well short of the size envisaged by Solomon. It was not Zerubbabel's fault, of course: the Temple's dimensions were determined by Cyrus and Darius, and the Jews were under their domination, followed by the Macedonian rule of Alexander and his successors. So this is not so much a new building project as the 'opportunity to restore this first archetype of piety to its former stature'.

Josephus himself seems both seduced by the grandeur of the successful project and repelled by Herod's manipulative rhetoric. This reaction is replayed again and again by modern historians too. Herod himself is repeatedly scorned as ambitious, violent and thoroughly undeserving of his sobriquet 'the Great'; the Temple, however, is celebrated and honoured as the second Temple, as if it were no more than the rebuilding of Solomon's first shrine, as Herod himself expressed his proposal, and as if Zerubbabel's Temple, which stood for 500 years, was somehow absorbed into Herod's design, rather than totally destroyed. The third Temple, according to orthodox Jews, will be built only when the Messiah comes, and when God orders it; for many Christians this will herald the Second Coming. For both groups it will mark the End of Days. So Herod's Temple is always known as the second Temple.

Herod's subjects, the Jews of Jerusalem, were also deeply ambivalent. They were dismayed at the prospect that Herod would tear down the existing Temple and then would not be able to complete the huge project. So Herod carefully promised not to start the work of destruction until all the materials and craftsmen for rebuilding were gathered. After this, we hear nothing but awe-struck wonderment at the completed building, and no nostalgia for Zerubbabel's shrine. Like the Book of Kings, even Josephus, no apologist for Herod, cannot resist the temptation of listing the sheer scale of the king's preparation: 'He prepared a thousand wagons to carry the stones, selected 10,000 of the most skilled workmen, purchased priestly robes for a thousand priests, and trained some as masons, others as carpenters ...' The sacred building was to be completed by the sacred hands of priests in all piety. Herod's project of kingly statecraft and pious architecture casts him as both David and Solomon.

The work began with the construction of the platform. It was supported by the great walls, 'the greatest ever heard of by man', as Josephus puts it. The walls were made of Jerusalem limestone and were mostly quarried nearby. The blocks are dressed on their outside face, and around the edges they have a chiselled border between 5 and 12 centimetres wide and about a centimetre deep. They were fitted together without mortar or bolts. Despite the pressure of retaining the Temple Mount, these walls have stood sturdily for 2,000 years. Part of the reason for their remarkable durability is the fact that the foundations were always dug to bedrock, even when the bedrock was some metres below the surface. Partly it is because of the stones' huge size. The smallest blocks (which are the majority) weigh between 2 and 5 tons. But there are several that weigh around 50 tons each, and the largest is around 12 metres long, 3 metres high, about 4 metres thick and weighs close to 400 tons. Figure 11 shows the excavation of the south wall, and it gives some sense of the size of the stones and the brilliance of the wall's construction. There is nothing like this anywhere else in the ancient world.

All monumental architecture sets out not just to amaze the spectator, but also to lead, direct and instruct. Great public buildings aim to *do* something to the citizen who stands before them and walks round them. Herod's Temple brilliantly used every architectural device to create a heightened feeling of religious community and invest the worshippers' religious experience with a sense of grandeur and focused intensity. Imposing gates led pilgrims through underground galleries to flights of steps that rose back out into the light. The pilgrims found themselves in a huge, high courtyard surrounded by tall porticos soaring above the mundane life of the city. Ahead stood the Temple itself, fenced off to keep out non-Jews. Beyond, each courtyard led further in towards the silent and forbidden Holy of Holies. As with a great stadium, the few entrances funnel individuals from the outside into a focused space, and construct a sense of a collected crowd, a community. The concentric courtyards also articulate a map of the different parts of the community – the outermost court for gentiles, the next for women, then Levites, then priests and finally the empty Holy of Holies – and each boundary fence increases the awe of the increasingly sacred. Figure 12 is a simple ground-plan which indicates the organisation of the Temple Mount – though it captures little of its astonishing impact. The Temple was a stunningly dramatic use of space.

Figure 13, a reconstruction based on the most recent archaeological evidence, gives a much better sense of the

[61]

11. Excavating at the foot of one of the retaining walls of the Temple Mount. The human figures give a good sense of the massive scale of the stones.

imposing stature of the project. The Temple Mount is pictured from the south-west and shows the entrances and porticos, though the Temple itself is not represented here. Centrally placed is a huge right-angled stairway rising directly to the portico. This is known now as Robinson's Arch, after the nineteenth-century American archaeologist Edward Robinson, who discovered the piers of the massive arch buttressing the wall. It was long assumed that this was the beginning of a huge bridge reaching over to the upper city across the valley beneath – it is as wide as a four-lane road – but archaeological discoveries in the dig which began in 1968 have conclusively shown that it was a kind of overpass that led up from the street and shops beneath. To the left on the Western Wall is a bridge to the upper city known today as Wilson's Arch (after its discoverer, a nineteenth-century English archaeologist), which some archaeologists think may actually have been a staircase also, like Robinson's Arch. To the right, however, on the southern wall are the two gates, the Hulda gates, through which the pilgrims entered, one with a double arch and one with a triple arch (though this has a much narrower staircase). There are also two small doors on the Western Wall at the same level. Figure 14 shows the staircase to the double door in the south wall, which was excavated only in the 1970s. This is a fine example of archaeology's ability to reveal the romance of stones. For the first time for centuries the steps over which countless pilgrims (including Jesus) would have entered the Temple have been laid open to view. Even the cynical may be touched by such a laden image.

The combination of archaeology's science and the artist's reconstruction gives us an evocative picture, but it conceals

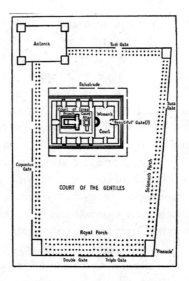

12. A plan of the Temple Mount.

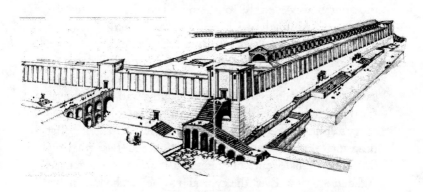

13. Leon Ritmeyer's image of the Temple Mount, seen from the south-west. Ritmeyer's picture is based on the most up-to-date archaeological information and is the most careful contemporary reconstruction.

pages of polemical argument. The question of how worshippers entered the Temple Mount is one of the most telling examples of how archaeology, history and religion vie for the same territory. There is a tractate of the Talmud called 'Middoth' ('Measurements') that reconstructs the details of the Temple's architecture. It is hard to date, though scholars usually think it was put in written form early as AD 150, that is, as little as seventy years after the destruction. It is explicit: 'There were five gates to the Temple Mount' – the two Hulda gates on the south; the Tadi gate on the north (which was not used); the Eastern gate and Coponius' gate on the west. The historian Josephus, however, who saw the Temple himself, says there were four gates in the Western Wall, and he mentions the bridge. Archaeologists indeed have found four entrances in the western side, although only two are gates on the same level as the Hulda gates (the two overpasses enter into the porticos). There is at least one further gate in the east wall, too, an exit from the vaults known as the Stables of Solomon (where the crusading Knights Templar stabled their horses). It is not easy to see how these descriptions can possibly be reconciled (though many have tried, especially religious archaeologists), and the failure of the Talmud to mention the western stairway entrances is baffling. Figure 12, the simple ground-plan of the Temple Mount taken from the French *Encyclopedic Dictionary of the Bible*, paradigmatically names five gates in line with the Talmud, and silently marks the other three entrances on the western side without discussion (and has no place for the eastern entrance to the vaults, which is bricked up today). It would seem that the gates not mentioned in the Talmud are treated as if they are without significance for the religious study of the Temple.

14. The southern staircase, uncovered by Mazar's dig. Pilgrims, including Jesus, would have entered the Temple up these stairs.

Pilgrims entered the street-level doors in the southern wall up the steps (there was a plaza outside to prevent crushing), proceeded along underground galleries and finally climbed stairs back into the light and the imposing scale of the Temple precincts. Covered porticos, held up by pillars, lined all four sides of the Mount. The Royal Stoa, the portico at the southern end above the Hulda gates, was the most impressive (Figure 13). It had three aisles that ran the whole length of the Temple Mount, made by four rows of pillars (162 in all), and it was strikingly high: anyone looking down from the rooftop into the ravine below 'would become dizzy and his vision would be unable to reach the end of so measureless a depth', as Josephus again wonderingly puts it; 'it was the most noteworthy structure under the sun'. The highly polished stone was lavishly decorated and the middle aisle was elevated into a double storey. The porticos made a frame for the huge open courtyard called the Court of the Gentiles. This was an area of unrestricted access and was designed to receive a huge number of people to observe the rituals of the Temple.

Temples were also places where money was banked, people met for business and, of course, there were stalls selling sacrificial animals: the porticos and this largest court made a crowded and bustling scene. Money-changers did brisk business: only the proper Hebrew currency, the 'holy shekel', could be used to pay the Temple taxes, so the other currencies of the empire needed to be exchanged at the tables set up in the porticos. (The word 'bank' is derived from *banca*, the term for a bench, or money-changer's table.) In the far corner of the Mount stood the Antonia, a fortress, named after Herod's protector Mark

Antony, which provided a military presence and a visible token of the power structures of the state – religion and politics have never been far apart in this corner of the world. The Temple Mount was also a citadel. There was a secret tunnel linking the Antonia with the Temple's inner court, 'in case the people turned against king'. There were thirty-four cisterns cut out of the rock underneath the Mount to receive the rainwater run-off; there was also an aqueduct to top up the system and an overflow passage, which led down to the pool of Siloam in the valley below. The system had a capacity of around 50 million litres, enough to withstand a serious siege. The size, organisation and strength of the site help explain why Titus' generals wanted to destroy it.

But to the north of all this bustle rose the Temple itself. For Herod, the huge height of Solomon's Temple recorded in Chronicles (120 cubits – 60 metres) – which modern scholars see as a textual error – was a claim to grandeur he was all too willing to live up to. The façade of his Temple soared a full 100 cubits – 50 metres – towards heaven.

The Temple, as the rules of purity in the Hebrew Bible suggest, was a space organised according to increasingly stringent ritual requirements, which were marked out physically by a set of bounded courtyards (Figure 15 gives a more detailed ground-plan). There was a balustrade round the whole Temple, a latticed fence made out of stone almost 2 metres high, according to Josephus (the Talmud gives a slightly lower height). This marked off the sanctified area, though it could be observed by the worshippers outside it. On the balustrade were signs written in Greek and Latin forbidding entrance to the inner courts to any gentile on pain of death (two of these signs in Greek have been discovered).

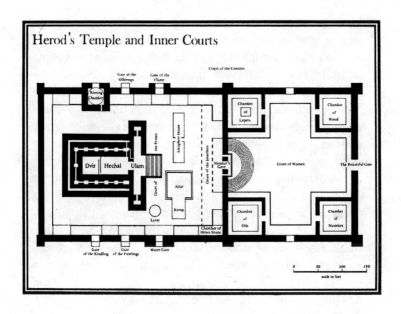

Herod's Temple and Inner Courts

Court of the Gentiles

Gate of the Offerings
Gate of the Flame

Rinsing Chamber

Chamber of Lepers
Chamber of Wood

Slaughter House

Dvir | Hechal | Ulam

the Porters

Court of

Nicanor's Gate
Court of the Israelites

Court of Women
The Beautiful Gate

Altar

Laver
Ramp

Chamber of Oils
Chamber of Nazirites

Chamber of Hewn Stone

Gate of the Kindling
Gate of the Firstlings
Water Gate

0   50   100   150
scale in feet

15. A plan of Herod's Temple.

[69]

Like most religious sites, the Temple practised a careful regulation of the insiders and the outsiders. It was structured, like Solomon's Temple, to lead through a series of rectangular courts to the innermost sanctum, and there were increasing levels of prohibition. The main entrance to the Temple itself opened into the Court of the Women. This was the area which Jewish women, along with men, were allowed to enter in order to participate in the religious ritual. There were four small square chambers, one in each corner of this courtyard: in two of them materials, wood and oil, were prepared for the sacrifices; in the other particular groups of men needing ritual purification, lepers and Nazirites, prepared themselves.

From the Court of the Women, steps rose to another single gate opening into the Court of the Israelites, an area open only to ritually cleansed Jewish males. In front of this was the Court of the Cohanim, the priests. There stood the slaughtering space where sacrificial victims were slaughtered, the altar where the victims were burnt, and the laver for ritual washing. Around the outside of this court was a corridor of rooms, with entrances to the outside courtyard: these rooms were used for the storage and preparation of wood, water, fire and animals for the ritual, which were brought in through the gates, named according to their use.

The Chamber of Hewn Stone however, the rabbis say, was used for meetings of the *cohanim*. Inside the inner Court of the Cohanim stood the Temple building itself. This was constructed according to the pattern of Solomon's Temple, with a porch (*ulam*), a hall (*hechal*) – into which only priests would go – and the Holy of Holies (*dvir*), into which only the High Priest went, and on only one occasion during the year, at the climax of the ceremonies of Yom Kippur, the Day of Atonement, the most solemn religious festival of the calendar. The pilgrims could only imagine what lay beyond the altar. The plan of the Temple led the *cohanim* and the minds of the worshippers upwards, through a series of gates and stairways, into increasingly sanctified areas, to the still, silent centre of the whole Temple complex: the empty Holy of Holies. The Temple was in its very structure an expression of religious order.

In its decoration, however, it was an astonishing statement of magnificence:

> *The outside of the building lacked nothing to astonish mind or eye. It was covered on all sides with massive plates of gold. When the sun came up, it radiated so fiery a flash that people had to avert their eyes as if they were looking directly at the sun. To strangers approaching from a distance it looked like a mountain covered in snow. Everything that was not gold was the whitest of white. On the roof there were sharpened gold spikes to stop birds perching and fouling it.*

All aspects of the Temple's interior are recorded in the same awe-struck way by Josephus, writing as a Jew to impress his Roman masters. The first gate, 35 metres tall, had no door, but its entire face was plated with gold: it drew in the visitor's eye towards the glittering *hechal*. (All the other doors were also plated with gold and silver, except for the Gate of Nicanor, which was of Corinthian bronze, and even more valuable.) Above the immense golden doors to the *hechal* were golden vines with grape clusters as large as a man. Inside the *hechal* was the seven-branched candelabrum, the tables on which the ritual loaves of bread ('the shewbread') were laid out each day, and the incense altar. In front of the golden doors (fully 20 metres high) hung a veil of Babylonian tapestry, embroidered in blue and red and purple and plain linen. For Josephus – and in this he is a typical educated pilgrim, although he also writes as a *cohen* himself, as he proudly tells us – the tapestry is an allegorical expression of the universe. The scarlet thread indicates fire, the plain linen the earth, the blue the air and the purple the sea. What was pictured on the tapestry was a view of all the heavens (but not the signs of the zodiac). The Temple is an expression of religious order, and its glorious decorations express God's handiwork both in their form and in their content. This allegorical reading of every aspect of the Temple becomes a commonplace of Jewish and Christian understanding. To view the Temple is always to see more than a material building.

BLOOD, FIRE AND TRUMPETS

The rituals which took place in this dazzling building are recorded at a level of detail that is unparalleled for any other ancient religious site. There were two daily services, morning and evening, with a third in the afternoons on the Sabbath, the New Moon and on the festivals, which attracted huge crowds into Jerusalem (the economy of the city was wholly dominated by this calendar). Individuals came to make offerings, too, in the times between services – sin offerings to expiate transgressions, to fulfil vows, or in thanksgiving.

Sacrifice was central to all of these occasions, and one of the things that is extremely difficult for a modern visitor to recapture is the overpowering *smell* of the ancient Temple. It would have been a heady mixture of incense (which was burnt on a small altar), together with the distinctive odours of fresh blood, slaughtered carcasses, animal dung, roasting meat and, no doubt, the smell of the crowd, all exacerbated by the heat of the sun in the open-air courts. At Passover, every family in the country was required to bring an offering of a lamb (the paschal lamb), which was slaughtered, roasted and consumed on the same day. The Talmud gives a figure for the number of kidneys roasted on such a festival (Agrippa, on behalf of the Romans, wanted the figures for a census of the Jews and the information is still used by literal-minded historians to calculate the number of families and thus the numbers of worshippers for a Temple festival). The figure is huge – 600,000 pairs of kidneys – and even if it only gives the vaguest sense of the real numbers (it is significantly noted to be twice the number of the Israelites who left Egypt in the Exodus), the noise and smell of slaughtering, skinning and roasting thousands of animals, with the detritus of hides and bones and dung, in the dazzle of the reflected light from the Temple's gold and polished stone walls, would have assaulted the senses. Which is why, no doubt, the Talmud lists as three of the miracles of the Temple that 'No woman miscarried because of the aroma of the sacrificial meat', that 'the sacrificial meat never became putrid', and that 'no fly was ever seen in the place where the meat was butchered'.

The priests, the *cohanim*, conducted the sacrifices. Priests and Levites came to live in the Temple on a rota; there were twenty-four groups, each of which served for a week at a time, twice a year. The priests travelled from their villages to serve with some ceremony and often with an escort. The daily sacrifice was carefully orchestrated, as were all the rituals. It began with the herald announcing that the sun had risen and it was time: 'The Priests should prepare for the service, the Levites for song and the Israelites for worship.' First, ash had to be cleared from the altar, since offerings were burnt on it at night. Lots were drawn for the honour (and there are stories of the good old days when young priests competed to be the first for this task). A full check of the site's religious paraphernalia was conducted, the fire prepared, and then the priests descended to the Chamber of Hewn Stone, where it was decided, again by lot, which priest would undertake which function in the sacrifice. A priest on the roof announced that light had spread in the sky as far as Hebron. The gold and silver vessels were laid out, the candlesticks were trimmed, and when the priest heard the great doors being opened, he began the slaughtering of the selected lamb, a perfect animal whose ritual suitability had been checked scrupulously. The animal's throat was slit, the blood was sprinkled against the altar and the animal butchered. The limbs were placed on the altar ramp, along with an offering of meal and oil and the High Priest's offering of a griddle cake, while the priests again went down to the Chamber of Hewn Stone to pray – prayers including the Ten Commandments, the Shema, still the most basic prayer of Judaism ('Hear, O Israel, the Lord is our God, the Lord is One') and blessings. Again lots were cast, and priests were selected to carry the incense into the sanctuary and the meat to the altar.

A huge gong was struck to announce the next stage of the ritual. The priests returned, cleared the inner altar, spread the coals and removed the ash-bin. As each finished his task, he prostrated himself and left the Temple sanctuary. They gathered on the steps of the porch, and then together pronounced the priestly benediction over the people who gathered for the ceremony in the courtyard. After the benediction, the offering was thrown on the altar, the meal offering was also sacrificed, and wine was poured out on appropriate places on the altar. Before the wine was poured trumpets blared, and during the libation cymbals were struck and the Levites sang the psalm of the day. (Levites were the singers in the Temple and also the guards, who manned the walls day and night.) At fixed points in the psalm, the trumpets blew again and the people prostrated themselves. The end of the psalm marked the end of the service.

This is as simple a description of the daily service as can be offered. Not only are there further intricate ritual activities prescribed, but also there is no point of the procedure that is not surrounded by precise and rigorous rules and made vivid by Talmudic discussion and collected lore. For example, the following paragraph taken from one of several collections of ritual laws (the Mishnah) gives detailed instructions for the priest who is chosen to clear the ashes from the altar:

He whose lot is was to clear the Altar of ashes went to clear the Altar of ashes, while they [the other priests] said to him, 'Take heed that you touch not the vessel [the silver firepan] before you have sanctified your hands and feet in the laver; and, lo, the firepan lies in the corner between the Ramp and the Altar, on the western side of the Altar'. None went in with him and he carried no lamp, but he walked in the light of the Altar fire. They neither saw him nor heard sound of him until they heard the noise of the wooden device which Ben Katin had made for the laver; and then they said 'The time has come!' He sanctified his hands and feet at the laver, took the silver firepan and went up to the top of

*the Altar and cleared away the cinders to this side and to that,
and scooped up the innermost burnt cinders and came down
again. When he reached the pavement he turned his face to the
north and went ten cubits to the east of the Ramp. He heaped the
cinders together on the pavement three handbreadths away from
the Ramp at the place where they throw the crops of the birds and
the ashes from the inner Altar and the Candelabrum.*

This one moment in the ceremony is precisely mapped
out, from where the ashes are placed to what the other priests
are expected to say. Worrying about the ritual precision,
talking about the rules, knowing that other people are also
worrying and talking about the performance are all as much
part of the ritual as the actions themselves.

The great festivals took this daily ritual to a new level of
engagement. The altar was cleared of ashes by midnight,
when the gates to the Temple court were opened. By dawn
the court was filled by pilgrims who came from all over the
country, and the priests, who also came from far and wide for
these occasions, gathered. For Passover, at least ten people
together offered a lamb. Because there were so many paschal
sacrifices, three groups of pilgrims entered the Temple court
in turn. The first group entered, and when the court was
filled, a ram's horn was blown. Priests stood in rows with gold
and silver basins (one row for gold, one for silver: it is integral
that where religion separates between profane and sacred,
impure and pure, each detail of the service makes visible the
boundaries of order). Each Israelite slaughtered his own
offering and the priest caught the blood in a bowl. The priest
passed back the full bowl to another priest, who passed him
an empty bowl for the next victim. The priest nearest the

altar poured the blood against the base of the altar. When the first group left, the second came in, and so on. Throughout the sacrifice, the Levites sang a fixed set of psalms, the Hallel (still sung on festivals in modern synagogues). The animals were roasted and eaten after nightfall for the Seder, the ritual meal, which was almost certainly the occasion of the Last Supper in the Gospels. Unleavened bread was eaten to remember the Exodus from Egypt, and no work was undertaken.

A festival such as Passover demonstrates how the Temple is integral to the construction of the Jews as a nation. The occasion celebrates the first foundation of the people as a people: according to the liturgy, the Jews came down to Egypt as a family, but they left Egypt as a 'great, mighty and prosperous nation'. It was on their journey from Egypt to the Promised Land that they were given the Torah, the law being observed in this ritual, and the Tabernacle, the very model of the Temple where they stand for the ceremony. From all around Palestine Jews gather to celebrate this exodus, and the very act of gathering together at the spiritual (economic, political) centre of Jerusalem is itself the act of making a community – showing the community to itself as a community. The shared ritual, culminating in a shared meal, further enhances the bonds of collectivity. The festival in the Temple is an axis around which national life revolved.

Perhaps the most impressive day of worship, however, was Yom Kippur, the Day of Atonement. This was the most solemn of occasions, marked by a complete fast for all the worshippers. This was the one day of the year on which the High Priest entered the Holy of Holies. Seven days before, he priest moved into separate quarters in the Temple

[77]

compound. He studied every detail of the ritual with the elders of the community (and again, the *study* of ritual is part of what makes it *tradition*: the passing on of lore as much as law). A deputy head priest was appointed, in case the High Priest died or was defiled in the night (any form of bodily emission would pollute the priest sufficiently to debar him from his duties). The Talmud earnestly and thankfully notes that the deputy was never actually required. On the Day of Atonement itself, the High Priest, in full regalia, performed all the duties of the daily sacrifice himself, undertook a series of ritual ablutions, then sacrificed a bull as his own sin offering and made a confession of his own and his family's sins, followed by the sins of the priests and the people of Israel. It was then that he uttered the holy name of God. The name, usually referred to by the Greek term Tetragrammaton ('word of four letters'), was only ever spoken by the High Priest and only on the Day of Atonement. When he pronounced the name, the people prostrated themselves and responded, 'Blessed be his name whose glorious kingdom is for ever and ever.' Solomon made a Temple of the Name of God, and at the central moment of the year's most awesome day, from the central, most holy spot in the Temple, the climax of ceremonial was the pronouncement of the name itself.

The service ended with another bizarre ritual (which has left its mark in most European languages). Two male goats were brought forward and the High Priest drew lots from a wooden box, one inscribed 'For Azazel' and the other 'A sin offering for the Lord'. The goat chosen 'For Azazel' was sent out of the Temple by a special door into the desert to die. The other was sacrificed as a sin offering, and the ceremony ended with an incense offering in the Holy of Holies and prayers for good weather and the security of the kingdom. The dismissal of a goat into the wilderness to bear away the sins of the community became a powerful symbol, particularly when Christianity developed its new idea of sacrifice, and the modern term 'scapegoat' in its much weakened metaphorical sense draws on this long tradition. This moment was, however, quite unlike any other ceremony in the Temple: no one quite knew what 'Azazel' meant, though as ever there are a string of rabbinical explanations and *midrashim* suggesting competing interpretations. Such inexplicable moments of symbolic action are easily absorbed into religious ritual: they become a crucial part of the establishment of tradition – 'this is what we do' – and with it the logic of the initiated insider's commitment to cultic activity.

The term 'sacrifice' today tends to be used to mean giving up a valued possession in the service of a greater good: men are sacrificed in the war effort, and so on. This reflects the pervasive influence of a Christian religious understanding. But in the Temple, sacrifice was a form of communication with God. There was certainly expense involved, and with a sin offering or a guilt offering the sacrifice came close to being a payment or punishment for transgression – or even a substitute for the sinner himself. But sacrifice was fundamentally an offering by man to the divine, which celebrated and honoured the divine, and marked the covenant between God and his people Israel: it expressed through ritual a sense of the order of the world (which is why ritual matters: a failed ritual is both a collapse of order and a failure of communication between man and the divine, with potentially disastrous consequences). As with other religions of the Mediterranean,

[79]

whether Greek, Roman, Egyptian or Eastern, sacrifice was an absolutely fundamental, regular and productive expression of religious life for Jews. Because the Temple had a monopoly on sacrifice in the Jewish kingdom, the destruction of the Temple by the Romans meant that the heart was ripped out of Jewish practice. The political, social and religious order which the Temple had provided was lost. What it meant to be a Jew – to live the life of a Jew – was no longer clear. It took centuries for this question to reach a stable answer (and some would say it has still not got there). Yet any such answer requires at least one thing: a new understanding of the Temple.

5

THE TEMPLE OF THE SCHOLARS:

A BUILDING OF WORDS

THE RELIGION OF THE BOOK

The destruction of Herod's Temple by Titus in AD 70 was total, but despite the immense power of the Roman Empire and the all-embracing political reach of the Romans' own polytheistic pantheon, not all Jews gave up hope of rebuilding their Temple. Despite the disastrous result of the revolt of 66, which led to the destruction of the Temple, in 132 the Jews again started a full-scale revolt against the Roman Empire, led this time by Bar Kochba. This revolt was also disastrous. Romans were masters of the politics of control. After the rebellion was crushed, Judaea was renamed Syria Palestina by the Romans (the first use of the word 'Palestine' for this area as a whole) to silence the connection between the land and the nation; the Temple Mount was ploughed over and a temple to Jupiter was built there, and the Jews were banned by imperial decree from entering Jerusalem. Jerusalem was now renamed Aelia Capitolina, and it was rebuilt along the Emperor Hadrian's template for a Graeco-Roman city. Caesarea – apt name – became the new political headquarters of what was a province now directly ruled by its Roman overlords.

The Bar Kochba revolt began optimistically, like many revolts. It minted its own coins. Coins were not merely the sign of an established central authority, they were also ways of representing the rulers to the people, and consequently coins are regularly part of the propaganda wars of ancient conflict. The Bar Kochba shekel had on one side the façade of the Temple. This image made a simple and direct rallying cry. This was a war to rebuild the lost Temple. On the reverse it shows the *lulav* and *etrog*, the branches and fruit that were carried at the festival of Sukkot (Tabernacles), the pilgrim festival celebrated at the Temple by the Jewish nation. Again, the imagery is easy to appreciate. These coins are tokens of a lost battle to restore the kingdom and the Temple.

There is a similar image of the Temple in a more surprising place. An ancient synagogue was excavated in 1932 in Syria, in a town called Dura-Europos. For some, it was a rather consternating discovery, for the synagogue was lavishly decorated with paintings. This seemed to contravene the express injunction of Exodus to make no graven image – and this law was in general observed by Jews, especially in the architecture of public, religious places. Moreover, the images themselves indicated an extensive interaction between Jewish and Greek artistic material. The discovery of the synagogue at Dura-Europos indicated that here was a community that had close integration with Hellenism (for all the talk of Judaism's rejection of Greek values) and did not observe the rules laid down so strictly by the rabbis (for all the talk of the authority of the rabbinate in the post-Temple period). Hence the consternation. Yet on the panel above the niche for the Torah scrolls there was a painting of the Temple which closely resembles the image on the Bar Kochba shekel. In

16. A shekel minted during the Bar Kochba revolt by the Jewish revolutionaries. The temple itself is on one side, and the *lulav* and *esrog*, plants carried during the rituals of *Sukkoth* [Tabernacles] in the temple on the other.

244–5, when this building was constructed and decorated, Herod's Temple was still a powerful symbol. The image shows the façade of the Temple with closed doors, which may be a significant indication of a sense of loss. Its position immediately above the scrolls may imply a connection between the Tabernacle as depicted in the five books of Moses, the Temple and now the synagogue. For already the synagogue as place of study and prayer had come to be seen as a replacement for – or continuation of – the Temple as the central focus of religious life.

The only practical attempt to reconstruct Herod's Temple comes from the least likely source: the Roman Emperor himself. Julian the Apostate came to power in the fourth century, after Constantine had converted to Christianity. Julian was, however, not Christian, and was passionately committed to a tradition of modern philosophy and pagan cult. His sobriquet 'the Apostate' was bestowed by the Christians, of course. In the two years of his rule (361–3) he attempted to reverse the policies of Constantine and his successors, but he died in battle before he could make a lasting impression. Julian himself writes in one of his letters that he intends to restore the Temple, no doubt as part of his attack on Christianity and its rejection of sacrificial cult. He appointed Alypius, the former governor of Britain, to oversee the work, but it failed almost before it had started. According to the Roman historian Ammianus, balls of fire burst out near the foundations and burned the construction workers. The project got no further. For Christian historians, this was an avenging fire from heaven, and they add that a cross mysteriously appeared in the sky, and cite other such miraculous signs. Sober modern writers choose either an earthquake or

17. An image of the temple painted on the wall of the synagogue in Dura-Europos in Syria. The temple, at the apex of the picture, seems to have its doors opening.

sabotage as the cause. Whatever the reason, after Julian's death there were no such further attempts. Rebuilding the Temple no longer functioned as a clarion call for political revolution. The Temple became a different lure and obsession – in the writings of the Talmud.

The Talmud consists in a collection of rules, the Mishnah, with extensive commentary on them, the Gemara. It is not a work of law, as it is sometimes depicted, but a work of discussion, story, argument and logic. (The text is now printed surrounded by further commentaries, as the work of debate continues over the centuries.) There are two traditions of the Talmud. The Palestinian Talmud was put together as an edited text in the late fourth century AD in Palestine; the Babylonian Talmud, composed in Babylon, was edited later, in the sixth to eighth centuries. They are independent texts, although they often have similar discussions of similar questions. Both Talmuds are the product of a much longer oral tradition and record discussions stretching back over many centuries. The Babylonian Talmud has come to be the dominant tradition in mainstream Judaism, and it is the Babylonian Talmud from which I cite in what follows. This is one of the most remarkable texts of the ancient world, and it stands at the crossroads of a social and intellectual development that is in itself an absolutely fascinating response to the destruction of the Temple.

When the Temple was destroyed, it was quite unclear what form Jewish religion should or would take. Without the central institution of sacrifice, the pilgrim festivals and the roles of the priesthood and Levites, the social and religious structure of worship was crushed. Synagogues had existed for many centuries as places of gathering for Jews, especially in the Jewish communities outside Palestine, where, along with a range of other social and intellectual activities, prayer took place (although prayer could and did take place anywhere, from private houses to the street or the workplace). By the time that the Talmud was written down in its edited form, the synagogue had become the prime focus of religious life. But what parts of Temple worship could take place in the synagogue? The Temple Mount is known in Hebrew also as *hamakom*, 'the place': the very spot is itself holy, and a Temple cannot be built anywhere else. There was, in fact, a temple built by Jewish mercenaries on the Egyptian island of Elephantinê which stands in the River Nile, in the fifth century BC. It appears that they, at least, thought there was nothing untoward about such a building, although when it was destroyed by fire in 410 BC it was not rebuilt. There was also, apparently, a temple at Leontopolis near Alexandria, established around 160 BC and destroyed on the instruction of Vespasian in AD 73 – but next to nothing is known of the purpose or practice of this foundation. The Samaritans, of course, built their temple on Mount Gerizim in competition with the Jerusalem Temple: it was destroyed by the Hasmoneans in 128 BC. But with the destruction of the Temple of Jerusalem, the issue became pressing: could sacrifice take place anywhere but on the altar at 'the place'? Could pilgrim festivals be observed away from Jerusalem and, if so, how?

The answers to such questions took many years and much debate, social disorder and discontinuity between communities to stabilise into a consensus. Sacrifice was not again performed: that means of communication between man and God was silenced. But the pilgrim festivals did continue in a changed form. On Sukkot, the *lulav* and *etrog*, the branches and fruit represented on the Bar Kochba shekel and which had been carried into and around the Temple precinct, were now carried around each synagogue. Passover no longer had the paschal sacrifice, but continued to hold the ritual meal of the Seder-night feast. But for neither, of course, did people leave their villages to travel to Jerusalem. The complex system of sin and guilt offerings was stopped, and how people thought about the relation between action and punishment had to alter radically as a consequence. Without a place for ritual cleansing, the rules of purity and pollution, fundamental to the Temple's drawing of boundaries and its sense of order, could no longer be maintained: people had to change their idea of how the body could be pure or defiled. After the destruction of the Temple, not only did a new religious expression of Judaism come about, but also a new sense of the religious self.

The role of the rabbis is integral to this development of what it means to be a Jew – and the notion of rabbi also changed fundamentally in this period. 'Rabbi' means 'my lord' in Hebrew, or 'sir'; it is not a priestly role, but an address which indicates someone who has the authority to make religious judgements and who teaches religious law. But with the growth of the importance of the synagogue and the search for a new form of Judaism, the rabbis began to take on an increasingly significant public position. Here too there is a myth of foundation. Yochanan ben Zakkai, a renowned sage in Jerusalem, like Jeremiah before him, saw no hope in opposing the invaders. He had some of his most talented pupils carry him out of the city in a coffin before the final sack of the Temple. He made his way to Vespasian, Titus' father, the Roman commander, whom he addressed as 'Caesar'. Vespasian, who was indeed shortly to become emperor, was flattered to be so addressed by the venerable authority, and granted Yochanan ben Zakkai's request to settle in Yavne, a village on the coastal plain. Here the rabbi settled down to establish a religious centre of learning and piety. The Sanhedrin became a rabbinical court here, and the rabbis provided the moral and religious leadership to a society shattered by the loss of the war with Rome.

This story is a classic charter myth that aims to create a continuous tradition from the distant past to the status quo of the current day, when rabbis did have considerable prestige and formal authority within Jewish communities. It even has the rabbi win over the future emperor, just as the stories have Alexander the Great prostrate himself before the High Priest. In reality, the Jewish society of Palestine was deeply fragmented by Roman imperialism and the dominance of Hellenic culture. In the towns, formal authority was invested in town councils (as with all Graeco-Roman towns in the East). Many Jews were integrated into the norms of Graeco-Roman culture, and the rabbis themselves record stories of men who tried to have an operation to reverse their circumcision in order to enter the gymnasium and bathhouse without seeming different. It is unclear how much influence rabbis had on the lives of Palestinian Jews, except for the few immediate students or followers. They performed religious rituals and taught, and were employed for these purposes in villages which could afford to do so and for people who wished it. There was a centre of learning at Yavne, but it is naïve to see it as the capital of a new Jewish kingdom led by scholars, as if the transition from the Temple to rabbinic Judaism was instantaneous, continuous and inevitable.

It is from this difficult time of dispersal and change that the Talmud takes shape. The Babylonian Talmud is an immense work of scholarly discussion. In each instance a piece of Mishnah, usually a regulation, or set of regulations, is set down, although even these regulations can contain differences of opinion within them ('X says such is the law, but Y says …'). Then the Gemara raises questions, explores difficult cases, tells stories, and constructs elaborate formal logical arguments about the implications of the rules. These debates are populated by a host of named rabbis both from before the destruction and from the first four centuries after the destruction, and the image presented is of immensely lively and influential rabbinical schools in earnest discussion at the centre of a bustling Jewish community. Rabbis emerge as saint-like performers of miracles and as petty squabblers, as pious scholars and carnal bodies, as parents and friends, as politicians and mystics. It is from the Talmud that the mythic picture of an ever-flowing rabbinic Judaism emerges. The Talmud offers a tradition that creates continuity instead of rupture: it is in this way, first of all, that the Talmud responds to the trauma of the destruction of the Temple. It imagines a lasting and immutable world of scholarly discussion that runs on whatever the historical circumstances.

Within the text of the Talmud, this idea of scholarly discussion is privileged in a manner quite distinct from Christian theology. There are a string of passages which discuss how to behave towards teachers, how to argue, what the formal rules of proof are, and there are splendidly vivid scenes which dramatise what happens when one rabbi differs from the majority opinion, or when dissent leads to arrogance or to violence, or when a student gets out of hand. Indeed, the Talmud explicitly states that it is not to be read by one person on his own, but always in the context of debate and discussion between at least two people. This is a text for arguing over, and not for solitary meditation or contemplation. It is a script which records discussion and demands that the discussion is reperformed with every reading. *Study* – collaborative study – becomes a cultural ideal. In rabbinic idealism studying the Talmud replaces the Temple: the proper service of God is to be found in the study-hall.

Indeed, in the Talmudic world picture, study even challenges prayer as the primary religious activity. As the synagogue became the hub of public religious expression, prayer became increasingly extended, significant – and discussed. Prayer service replaced the sacrificial service. This finds strikingly bold expression:

> *When Rav Sheshet was engaged in a fast, he spoke thus after praying: 'Master of the Universe, it is revealed before You that at the time when the Holy Temple stood a person who sinned would offer a sacrifice, and he would offer from it only its fat and blood, and that alone would atone for him. And now, when there is no Temple, I have engaged in fasting and my own fat and blood have been diminished. May it be Your will that my fat and blood that are diminished be regarded as if I had offered them before You on the Altar, and may You do me favour.'*

The rabbi's prayer and his own bodily substance have become a novel form of sacrifice now that the Temple no longer stands.

The three daily prayer services stand in for the three sacrificial services, therefore. But the Talmud also invents an even older and more august tradition to explain where prayer service comes from. Rabbi Yose, son of Rabbi Chanina, argued that the three prayer services were established by the three Patriarchs: Abraham, Isaac and Jacob. 'Abraham instituted the morning prayer, as it is stated (Genesis 19.27), "And Abraham arose early in the morning to the place where he had stood". "Standing" refers to nothing other than prayer.' This is a typical piece of exegesis. Abraham is declared to have started the tradition of morning prayer, and this is proven by a biblical verse. The verse at first sight has nothing to do with prayer; but, as the Talmud goes on to show, there are other biblical verses where 'to stand' implies 'to stand in prayer'. Abraham also goes to 'the place', which helps form an association with the Temple. So the verse is the first and foundational example of morning prayer. So when Genesis states (24.63), 'Isaac went out to contemplate in the field towards evening', this refers to the afternoon prayer, since 'contemplate' can mean 'to address God in prayer'. And Jacob 'came upon the place and spent the night there' (Genesis 28.11). 'The place', despite this being the narrative of Jacob's travels, is understood in a heightened religious sense. This founds the practice of the evening prayer. By this process of interpretation the origin of prayer services is taken back to the very beginnings of religious history. The Temple services themselves are built upon this platform. The Talmud's desire to find continuity could not be more strikingly demonstrated. With a wilful twisting of history, it sets out to prove that the prayer services which replaced sacrificial ritual after the destruction of the Temple were not only always present in Judaism, but were actually the origin of the sacrifices themselves. How things are today is how things always have been.

Prayer replaces sacrifice as the key form of communication with God, but the Talmud makes prayer a subject for highly involved discussion too. Prayer must be performed in a particular way, and it is only by study that you can find out how to stand, what to say, with what feelings a prayer should be uttered, what to do if you miss out a word, or, to take another example from the Talmudic tractate Berachot, what to do if you are travelling by donkey in a caravan and it is impossible for you to get off to stand in the normal way, and you are not sure in which direction Jerusalem lies, but the time for prayer arrives. What these discussions reflect is not merely a searching for a protocol to replace the ritual of the Temple but a debate between rabbis about which is more important: prayer or study. Both prayer and study, however, are performances to replace Temple ritual in the new, post-destruction community.

Most remarkable, however, is the Talmud's attempt to make the Temple live on in its pages. The Tractate Middoth, 'Measurements', which atypically has no discussion (*gemara*), rehearses the measurements of Herod's Temple, cubit by cubit, and runs through the map of the building, recording the use of different rooms. It is an act of remembrance made poignant especially by such comments as this little discussion between two rabbis:

'As for the south-western small chamber,' said Rabbi Eliezer ben

Yaacov, 'I forget what it was used for.' Abba Saul says, 'They used to store there wine and oil. And it was called the oil storage rooms.'

The map is not merely laid out for us: it is staged as a threat of forgetting defeated by an act of memory. To study is to memorialise the destroyed Temple.

This study of the lost and idealised past becomes an obsessive activity. Tractate Nazir looks at every aspect of the rites of the Nazirite. A Nazirite was a man who vowed not to drink wine or cut his hair for a certain number of days as a form of self-dedication: the procedure is described very briefly in the Book of Numbers. At the end of the period of the vow, the Nazirite had to go to the Temple, cut his hair and offer a sacrifice to mark the end of the ritual period. This was a minor and rather extreme religious activity which became impossible to practise with the destruction of the Temple. None the less, there is a lengthy tractate arguing about every detail of the ritual – from whether the vow is valid if the man slips and says 'Pazir' instead of 'Nazir', to the detailed ritual rules for the final sacrifice in every conceivable test case (and some rather unlikely test cases). The performance of argument takes over from any possible practical instruction for day-to-day life. None of the rituals of the Nazirite could be performed any more. Discussing the now impossible Temple ritual becomes a new form of religious self-expression.

In the final twist of this process, the prayer services themselves start to follow this particular logic of memorialisation. The afternoon service of Yom Kippur, the Day of Atonement, in the Temple included the High Priest's sacrifice and confession, described earlier. After the destruction of the Temple, however, the service took the form of a description of the ceremony that used to be performed, which gradually was lengthened by the addition of poems and hymns that extolled and idealised all aspects of the ceremony. ('The priest would take the blood and sprinkle it on the altar and he used to say …') The poets tried to make the occasion as vivid as possible, and poetic creativity produced some finely imagined responses. The Temple service cannot be performed so it is recalled in creative poetry; this poetry itself becomes the new ritual. The ceremony here is a ritual performance of a myth about a ritual performance: a Temple service of the imagination.

After the destruction of the Temple, prayer service and study replaced the ritual of the Temple. Studying the Talmud became a way of memorialising the Temple – reconstructing it in the mind. This intellectual activity became an integral part of the self-definition of rabbinical Judaism, and became institutionalised in religious services. The Temple became a monument of the imagination.

6

....

YOUR BODY IS A TEMPLE

GLORIFY GOD WITH YOUR BODY!

Christianity began as a minor rebellious sect of Judaism and it spent a great deal of energy distinguishing itself from Judaism, a process that took a long time and no little pain. It should not be a surprise, then, to see Christianity both at its beginning and throughout its history adopting and adapting the image of the Temple to its own agenda. As a Jew, Jesus went to the Temple to teach and to worship – it was a natural and expected destination for him; so too did Paul, though he got into trouble for trying to take a non-Jew past the boundary into the inner court. But surprisingly, with the exception of Jesus' prophecies in the Gospels, early Christians do not discuss the destruction in any detail at all; rather, Christianity sets out to redefine the Temple and create a more polemical and novel sense of the House of the Lord. Later Christian historians found the destroyed Temple a perfect and satisfying example of the punishment of the Jews. But it was Paul who most influentially and most interestingly changed the idea of the Temple for Christians. He demanded that they find a new way to understand the perils of defilement and the joys of purity. What has now become a tired metaphor was originally a powerful piece of religious polemic. When Paul declared, 'your body is a temple', he was aggressively marking the unique theology of Christianity.

'Think not that I have come to abolish the law and the prophets', says Jesus in the Gospel of Matthew. 'I have come not to abolish them but to fulfil them.' The first generation of Christians do seem to have taken part in Temple ritual with its battery of laws, but soon the more aggressive separation of Christianity from Judaism and from Graeco-Roman society demanded a more radical attitude towards the Temple's central rite of sacrifice. The 'fulfilment' of sacrifice (along with other central rites such as circumcision and dietary regulations) came to mean the refusal of any physical performance, coupled with a new metaphorical, spiritual understanding of the term. 'I am come to destroy sacrifice,' says Jesus in the Gospel of the Ebionites. This is the boldest and most blunt statement of a crucial strand of early Christianity's comprehension of the Temple (for all that the Gospel of the Ebionites never made it into the canon). Animal sacrifice was the central ritual of Greek and Roman religion (as it was in the Temple). The rejection of the ritual and cult of both the Temple and of Graeco-Roman religion was a gesture that defined the Christians and separated them from the culture of the Roman Empire as much as from the culture of Judaism. A Christian had to refuse to participate in sacrificial ritual.

The martyrs are the heroes and saints of early Christianity, men and women who gave their lives to testify to their love of God and commitment to Christianity (martyr means 'witness'). Early Christian texts revel in the triumph of these figures: the Acts of the Martyrs, the Lives of the Saints, the hymns of honour for the martyrs are texts that celebrate

Christianity's militant self-display, and were read publicly and privately to encourage their audiences to the exhibition of faith. Again and again it is the refusal to take part in the ritual of sacrifice that leads to martyrdom. Here is Prudentius, a fourth-century Latin poet from Spain, extolling the martyrdom of St Vincent, who would not join in the pagan sacrifices:

> The minister of idolatry,
> Girded with grim laws,
> Sought to compel you with steel and chains
> To sacrifice to the gods of the nations.
> First he softly spoke
> Wheedling words of persuasion,
> Like a wolf on the hunt,
> Which first toys with the calf
> It is going to ravish:
> 'The Greatest Sovereign of the World', he said,
> 'Who wields the sceptre of Rome,
> Has ordained that all the world shall serve
> The ancient rites of the gods.
> Attend, Nazarene,
> Spurn your crude observance.'

Vincent duly refuses to participate in the sacrifice, and we are treated to 500 lines of gory description of torture, as the saint laughs at his torturer's attempts to hurt him through his mortal flesh. All forms of ritual sacrifice are despised and rejected, and must be seen to be so spurned. A saint such as the young woman Eulalia even had to run away from home in order to thrust herself into a position where she could publicly refuse 'to burn incense and offer burnt sacrifice of the livers of cattle to gods who bring death'. In her house in the countryside with her caring mother, there was no opportunity to win the crown of martyrdom. Such a rejection of sacrifice was a clear public demonstration of the Christian's wilful self-exclusion from the norms and bonds of society. Where the sacrificial festivals of the Temple were occasions for the maintenance and assertion of a sense of community, the Christians found brotherhood through rejecting the values of the community, even to the point of a willed death.

The Gospels were a spur to such a negative view of the Temple and its cult. Jesus dismissed his followers' admiration for the stones of the Temple with a prediction of their destruction: the pointedness of this exchange is doubly highlighted now that we have seen how the production and the size of the stones are both commonplaces of awe-struck praise by Greeks, Romans, Jews – and modern archaeologists. Jesus is also represented as throwing the money-changers out of the Temple because their materialism falls short of the spiritual values of the holy place. He also criticises the legal restrictions of the expert exegetes of the law in the Temple, and finally promises the disciples that his resurrection after three days would inaugurate a new Temple: 'Destroy this Temple and in three days I will raise it up again' (John 2). This prophecy sees the architectural Temple replaced by Jesus himself. Indeed, what the Hebrew Bible says about the foundation of the Temple is applied throughout the Gospels to the figure of Jesus Christ: it is through Jesus that man will now experience the presence of God.

Yet the positive valuation of the language of sacrifice does remain in the figure of Jesus Christ: this is how for

Christians the law of sacrifice is 'fulfilled'. The death of Jesus is represented as a willed loss for a greater good, a sacrifice in the modern sense – indeed the primal sacrifice where one death brings eternal life for the world. After Jesus, there is no need any more for sacrifices. The image of the Lamb of God plays its role here too. The Lamb evokes not merely peacefulness, gentleness and the Shepherd of the people, but also the sacrificial lamb, the offering at Passover, which was the time of the Crucifixion. The death of Jesus, together with the rejection of Temple ritual, fundamentally alters the notion of sacrifice in the Christian tradition. The Crucifixion of Jesus is the sole sacrifice, which is to be understood as the grandest of theological concepts: a death that brings the hope of eternal life for men. The Temple's central ritual metamorphosed into the central theological concept of the new religion.

The image of the Temple itself developed as Christianity grew in power and numbers of believers. As Christians began to form communities in the eastern Mediterranean and beyond, the Temple as the site of collective worship was taken up as a positive expression for Christian communal values. Paul sets the tone as he encourages the Corinthians:

> *Do not be misyoked with unbelievers. For what fellowship exists between righteousness and lawlessness? Or what communion of light with darkness? What accord exists between Christ and Beliar, or what portion has a believer with an unbeliever? What agreement exists between the Temple of God and idols? For we are the Temple of the living God; as God said 'I will dwell in them and move among them, and I will be their God and they will be my people'.*

Paul appeals for a separation between the righteous and the unrighteous, the believer and the unbeliever: this will be a 'cleansing from every defilement of body and spirit'. As the architectural Temple articulated and maintained boundaries between the pure and the impure, the holy and the secular, so Paul's rhetoric seeks to divide the pure, holy Christian from the defilement of the non-Christian. Hence the Temple appears as the central image to hold his argument together: but now the Temple *is* the community, a Temple of men: 'we are the Temple'. The rejected and destroyed physical Temple of the Jews is reborn as a spiritual community. 'The place', *hamakom*, 'the House of the Name of the Lord', can now be reconstructed anywhere 'where men gather in My name'.

Paul's language here seems strikingly to echo the Dead Sea Scrolls, the holy scriptures of the group of Essenes at Qumran. In their exclusion from the Temple itself at Jerusalem this religious sect regarded their own community as replacing the Temple. They saw themselves as a spiritual group whose purity would lead to the fulfilment of the prophecy of a new Temple. Early Christians were drawn towards the Essenes' extreme attitudes towards purity and sexual abstinence – and it is typical of the complexity of the birth of Christianity that we find the ideas of this extreme Jewish sect strongly influencing an apostle who is so influential in the church's rejection of the basic practices of Judaism such as circumcision and dietary laws.

The influence of the Essenes' hostility to the fleshly body is also evident in Paul's writing as he shifts the conception of the Temple still further. Paul aggressively attacks the Corinthians for their sexual immorality. Corinth was a city where the Greek temple was famously said to house sacred prostitutes, and he wants Christians to have nothing to do with such licence. 'Do you not know that he who joins himself to a prostitute becomes one body with her? For, as it is written, "The two shall become one flesh". But he who is united to the Lord becomes one spirit with him. Shun sexual immorality!' The Greek word I have translated 'sexual immorality' – the standard translation here is simply 'immorality' – is *porneia*, which implies the manifestation of desire for another person's body, especially in the context of prostitution and other pursuits of sensual pleasure. It is sometimes translated 'fornication' (it is the root of the English word 'pornography'). *Porneia* will constitute a major worry of Christian moralists. Paul continues:

> *Every other sin that a man commits is outside the body. But the sexually immoral man sins against his own body. Or do you not know that your body is a Temple of the Holy Spirit inside you, which you have from God? You are not your own. You were bought with a price. So glorify God with your body.*

This concludes a remarkable argument. Paul moves from criticising men who have sex with prostitutes (an easy enough moral stance) to lauding a spiritual union with God (a far harder idea). It would seem – and this is the hardest idea of all – that the physical union of bodies in sex prevents a spiritual union with the Lord. Significantly, the next chapter of the Letter will praise the state of virginity as the ideal for men and women, while allowing lawful marriage only a very restricted place as a way of stopping the lustful from burning in hell for the sin of fornication. A fundamental command of God in Genesis is 'Go forth and multiply', but here such a message has been replaced by an allegorical spiritual wedding with Christ, which will find its institutional form in the later monasteries of virgin men and nunneries of virgin women. The image on which the argument rests is once again the Temple, but now the Temple has been transformed into each Christian's body, in which the Holy Spirit dwells. Each man and woman must use his or her body to glorify God, as the Temple was used to glorify God. The sexual purity of the body has become the defining category of holiness. When your body joins with another's in sexual congress, it is like the defiling of the Temple. The Temple, a holy place defended by rules of purity, becomes a grounding metaphor for the Christian obsession with the purity and sullying of the *flesh*.

These radical theological reconstructions of the idea of the Temple help explain why the Christians did not attempt to rebuild the Temple on the Temple Mount. The physical Temple had been replaced with a spiritual community or with an individual's own sexual purity. Christ's sacrifice meant that animal sacrifice was no longer required. For Helena, the mother of Constantine, and for Constantine and the later Christian emperors, the empty Temple Mount testified to Jewish error, transcended by the new religion. So Saint Jerome at the end of the fourth century describes how a few Jewish pilgrims struggled to Jerusalem to lament the anniversary of the destruction: 'You see a sad people coming, decrepit little women and old men encumbered with rags and years, exhibiting in their bodies and their dress the wrath of the Lord … they are not worthy of pity'. The Jews had been punished by God for their failure to accept Jesus as the Messiah, and the destruction of the Temple remained the visible sign of that punishment, just as the purity of Christians and the piety of their community were the new Temple of the Lord. There was simply no need for a building. Or rather, there was a need for no building.

This rejection of the physical Temple did not last. Anicia Juliana was a fabulously wealthy princess of the Byzantine royal family who built the Church of St Polyeuktos in Constantinople around 525. It was a huge and splendid edifice. A poem inscribed in the church proclaimed without any trace of humility that she had 'surpassed the wisdom of Solomon, raising a Temple to God'. Archaeologists have duly discovered that the building was 100 cubits long by 100 cubits wide (or thereabouts, if you allow for the inaccuracy of building techniques). In the Christian empire, the politics of conspicuous consumption led its rulers to compete even with the kings of the Bible. The celebrated Emperor Justinian, who built Hagia Sophia, the very greatest of Byzantine churches, in Constantinople, wanted to trump both the past and the example of Anicia Juliana. When Hagia Sophia was completed, the story goes that he declared, 'Solomon, I have surpassed you' (as every tour guide will tell you). Constantine had built the Church of the Holy Sepulchre expressly 'to surpass the excellences of every city'. Justinian goes even further by challenging Solomon's Temple itself. The Temple has become a physical, architectural model to be followed and even bettered.

Later Christianity certainly had its architectural ambitions, though they are rarely expressed with quite the triumphal competitiveness with the biblical past that Justinian displays. The soaring cathedrals of the medieval period were built to the glory of God (though no doubt with half an eye on the fame of their sponsors). The Temple is a distant ideal for these masterpieces, though some scholars have searched hard – sometimes rather too hard – to find the pattern of Ezekiel's Temple in, say, the proportions of Salisbury Cathedral. Since the building itself – roughly in the shape of a cross – has little obvious physical resemblance to the ancient Temple, it is only by looking at mathematical ratios that the link can be made. (Obsessiveness about measurement seems to go hand in hand with a fascination with the Temple.) But the pull of the glorious depiction of the Temple in the biblical texts was hard to resist, and medieval and Renaissance Christians continued to read the descriptions of Solomon's Temple, Ezekiel's vision and Herod's monument with passion and intensity – and to reconstruct the building itself with the mind's eye. They drew picture after picture, imagining a rebuilt temple, as we will see in chapter 8. But they also used the Temple as a model on which to build their own understanding of the world. The Temple returns as a positive image for Christian thinking.

John Bunyan, who most famously wrote *The Pilgrim's Progress*, also produced in 1688 a less distinguished volume called *Solomon's Temple Spiritualized*, which in its style of allegorical reading is all too typical of many other works in the modern Western European Christian tradition from the Venerable Bede's *On Solomon's Temple* onwards. The Talmud already had interpreted the Temple in this way: 'The Temple corresponds to the whole world and to the creation of man who is a small world', it writes. Each element of the Temple, that is, corresponds to the world – so the candelabrum's seven lights correspond to the seven stars – and also correspond to a part of man – so the golden altar corresponds to the soul of man and the brass altar to the body of man. Josephus and, before him, Philo, the Jewish philosopher who lived in Alexandria, created longer allegorical explanations of the Temple for their sophisticated Greek readers. Bunyan's book offers fully seventy chapters of such symbolic geography, which can seem painfully strained to modern readers, for all that he is trying hard to stick to good Protestant straightforwardness in his clear and forthright prose.

Take the golden spoons in the Temple, one of the less-imposing ritual accoutrements. He discourses on them at length, expanding the conceit that spoons are used for feeding babies, and that we are all Babes in Christ, who are provided for by the Nurses of the Church, that is, the ministers – and so on for two pages. Every architectural element or ritual object proves to be a 'type' – a prior model – of Christian spirituality: this typological reading takes the reader on a tour of the Temple, proving the Christian significance of every detail. It is a way of creating a symbolic world, and of encouraging the reader to find a Christian message all around him. Bunyan wants the reader to learn how to view everything in the world as a sign of God's order. The Temple is a guide for looking at the world through Christian eyes.

When Christian theologians write history, it tends to be history that culminates in the triumph of Christianity. This constantly affects how the Temple is viewed. As late as the nineteenth century books were being printed with titles such as this mouthful from George Holford: *The Destruction of Jerusalem: an absolute and irrefutable proof of the divine origin of Christianity including a narrative of the calamities that befell the Jews so far as they tend to verify our Lord's prediction relative to that event, with a brief description of the city and the Temple.* From this it can probably be guessed that the book sees the destruction of the Temple as 'the condign and predicted punishment' of 'the exasperated bigotry of the Jews', though the real enemies of the polemic are the modern rational thinkers of the Enlightenment who attack religion.

But the story of the Temple's loss need not be one of punishment: it can express an inevitable and easy transcendence. Ernst Lohmeyer, one of the most distinguished modern German theologians, who was executed by the communists in post-war Germany, writes, 'Wherever the Christian Gospel has taken root ... temple and sacrifice have disappeared from the land and the life of the people ... Attacks on temples by the early Christians and throwing down of altars are almost unknown. The sacrifices simply go out like a fire that is not tended, the altars disappear.' This is a shockingly misleading denial of how Christian authorities violently suppressed pagan and Jewish religion in antiquity and afterwards. But it takes on an even grimmer aspect when it is revealed that it was written while the author was serving as a pastor in the Nazi army on the eastern front. The historian is always implicated by his place in history.

For Christianity, the history and the theology of the Temple are deeply intertwined – in what can seem a rather paradoxical doubleness. On the one hand, Christians celebrated the destruction of the Temple as the triumph of Christianity over Judaism: God's punishment of the religion that did not accept Jesus. On the other hand, Christians elevate the Temple as an image of spiritual order. The Temple becomes Christ, the community of Christians, the Christian's body and even a model for the Church. The new Temple is fundamental to Christianity, and finding how the Temple is to be remade is a defining Christian activity.

7

CALIPHS AND CRUSADERS

THE NIGHT JOURNEY TO JERUSALEM

The prophet Mohammed died in Medina in 632. The army of his followers, led by Caliph Omar ('Umar), had defeated the Christian Byzantine forces in Syria, conquered Damascus and by 638 were already at the gates of Jerusalem. It was an astoundingly swift and successful expansion, which would continue all the way to Spain. The Christian patriarch Sophronios, with no military support from Byzantium, rapidly agreed to surrender the city to Omar in person and, with a spectacular gesture of respect that only someone of uncontested power could make, Omar entered the city on foot, dressed in a simple camel-hair tunic.

Islamic religion, like Christianity and Judaism, did not spring forth fully armed, but was a system which developed over many years through internal conflicts, external pressures and theological debate. And, as with Christianity and Judaism, Jerusalem and the Temple Mount play an integral role in this history. Abraham is the father of Muslims (as he is of Jews and Christians); Jesus is recognised as a prophet by Muslims too. Following this sense of tradition, Caliph Omar allowed Jews to return to Jerusalem, and granted Christians free use of their holy sites. The tenth-century Islamic geographer al-Muqaddasi, who praises Jerusalem as 'the most sublime of cities', notes the results of this policy rather more dyspeptically: 'Few are the learned there, many are the Christians, and these make themselves distasteful in the public spaces ... The Christians and the Jews are predominant here, and the mosque devoid of congregations and assemblies.' Caliph Omar's openness helped make Jerusalem the city it is still today: an intense collocation of Jews, Christians and Muslims.

Jerusalem is the third most holy city of Islam after Mecca and Medina. Its holiness is established by a variety of sacred texts – the Qur'an first of all, of course, and with it the stories of the life of Mohammed passed down originally in oral form and collected as *hadith*. Like *midrashim* in the Jewish tradition, works of *hadith* are stories that respond to exegetical problems in the Qur'an, and they have become authoritative texts for the formation of Muslim cultural identity, as well as being the foundational stories about the first generation of Mohammed's followers and Mohammed himself. Like *midrashim*, their historical basis is much questioned by modern critical scholarship, but, even more than the *Midrash*, they play a central role in the construction of the faith of the faithful. The second *surah* (roughly, 'chapter') of the Qur'an itself, however, provides the first claim for Jerusalem's holiness. When Mohammed fled from Mecca to Medina, he thought he would make Jerusalem the place towards which one must face to pray – the *qibla*. But in the second year of the flight (*hegira*), after an argument with the Jews of Medina, Mecca was chosen as the *qibla*, and so it has remained.

Nasir al-Khusrau, a Persian Muslim who travelled to Jerusalem in 1047, writes an account of his response to the

sacred rock in the Dome of the Rock, the octagonal shrine on
the Temple Mount built precisely to house it, which vividly
demonstrates how these religious texts structure the percep-
tion of a faithful viewer:

> *This stone of the Sakrah is that which God commanded Moses to*
> *institute as the* qibla ... *Then came the days of Solomon – upon*
> *him be peace! – who seeing that the Rock was the* qibla *built a*
> *mosque around it [the first Temple] ... So it remained until the*
> *days of our Prophet Mohammed, the Chosen One – upon him be*
> *blessings and peace! – who likewise recognized this to be the*
> qibla, *turning towards it at his prayers; but God – be He exalted*
> *and glorified! – afterwards commanded him to institute as the*
> qibla, *the house of Ka'aba [at Mecca].*

When Nasir al-Khusrau looks, he sees in the Rock the
religious history of the site from Moses to his own day, a
history which stresses the continuity of the prophetic tradition instantiated in this one spot, and the revolutionary
moment of Mohammed's revelation. For this pilgrim, it is
essential to his experience that the Dome of the Rock
replaces the Temple of Solomon, as Islamic religion replaces
the Judaism and Christianity which preceded it.

The holiness of this site for Islamic thinking, however,
stems especially from the *hadith* and from biographies of
Mohammed, written in the eighth century and later, which
expand on the seventeenth *surah* of the Qur'an, known
usually by the title 'The Night Journey'. The Qur'an gives
only the briefest narrative of how Mohammed was carried
'from the sacred temple to the temple which is more remote,
whose precinct we have blessed, that we might show him of

our signs …'. This typically opaque and non-specific language of revelation is given a more precise geography, which focuses on the Temple Mount, by Ibn Ishaq, the first biographer of Mohammed who writes in the eighth century, 'then the Messenger of God was carried by night from the Mosque of the Ka'aba to the Aqsa Mosque, which is in the Holy House of Aelia [Jerusalem]'. The story is expanded further by Ibn Ishaq and others. The angel Gabriel came in the night to where Mohammed was sleeping, took out his heart, purified it and filled the cavity with faith and science. He kicked Mohammed awake (according to a later elaboration, recorded by Ibn Hisham in the name of Al-Hassan, Gabriel has to kick him three times before Mohammed sees what he needs to see). Gabriel brought him outside and there was a white animal, between a mule and a donkey in size, with wings – al-Burak. With Gabriel as a guide, Mohammed was transported to Jerusalem by the animal, where he found Abraham, Moses, Jesus and the company of prophets in the Temple. Two bowls were given to Mohammed, one with milk, the other with wine. He drank from the bowl of milk, and Gabriel praised him: 'You have been guided to the true religion, and your community will be so guided. Wine is forbidden to you.' (Hence Muslims do not drink alcohol.) When Mohammed returned to Mecca, most people did not believe he could have made such a journey in one night, but Abu Bakr recognised the truth of it, and testified that Mohammed was the Messenger of God.

The story goes on with Mohammed saying how he rose from the Temple Mount to heaven, on a ladder of the finest gold. He rose through the seven heavens to the seat of God. He saw the sinners being punished: 'I saw men with lips like camels, with pieces of fire like stones in their hands. They thrust them in their mouth and they came out of their posteriors. Gabriel told me these are those who sinfully devour the property of orphans.' He also sees the prophets as he rises: Jesus, Moses, Aaron and Abraham. Finally from God he receives the rule that Muslims are to pray five times a day. The 'night journey' – from Mecca to Jerusalem to the seventh heaven – is celebrated in the Islamic festival of Lailat al Miraj, when the story is recounted.

Jerusalem and the site of the Temple in Jerusalem are holy because of the miraculous journey from Mecca ('Mecca and Jerusalem are constantly linked', as one commentator puts it), and because it was from this site that Mohammed brought the rules which are so important to the cultural and religious self-definition of Muslims: the duty of daily prayer and abstinence from alcohol.

As the stories of the 'night journey' grew in number and richness, so too did the response to the site itself. Caliph Omar, as we've already seen, made the Patriarch Sophronios crawl through the refuse on the deserted site, a humiliation to redress the humiliation of the holy site, and began the process of restoration. He built a large but simple mosque, little more than a four-square wooden building, but capable of housing 3,000 worshippers. It was the Caliph Abd al-Malik who built the Dome of the Rock fifty years later in 691 (although it has often been wrongly called the 'Mosque' or 'Dome of Omar' by Western travellers). The Dome still dominates the skyline of Jerusalem. It has been restored many times, most significantly in the sixteenth century by Suleiman the Magnificent, the Ottoman sultan, who covered it with its beautiful mosaic of tiles, and, more recently in the twentieth century, when the

18. The Dome of the Rock, with the sun glittering off its burnished roof.

roof was restored with a glittering alloy that shines like gold in the bright daylight.

The Dome of the Rock was built, according to the authorised exegesis, to commemorate the 'night journey' of Mohammed. The Rock itself is honoured as the spot of three famous moments of the Hebrew scriptures: it is the altar of Solomon, the site of the binding of Isaac, and the place where King David asked God forgiveness for his sins. On the Temple Mount there are also other memorials of particular moments in the night journey: one spot is honoured as 'the station of Burak', where the steed was tethered. The other mosques on the site also memorialise passages from Holy Scripture. The al-Aqsa Mosque was built by Abd al-Malik's son, al-Walid. The Qur'an spoke of Mohammed going to 'the far mosque' (*al-Aqsa*). The al-Aqsa Mosque, when it was built, turned that rather vague reference into a visible and permanent building on the Temple Mount. (The foundations of the al-Aqsa were also said to have been laid by King David, adding a further genealogy to the site.) The grotto under the rock itself shows where the rock tried to rise with Mohammed into heaven, as the indentation on top of the rock shows where Mohammed's foot kept it attached to the earth. To walk on the Temple Mount is to walk on the buried life of stories.

The Dome is truly beautiful. As al-Muqaddasi eloquently put it in the tenth century, 'This is a marvel to behold, and one such that in all Islam I have never seen its equal; neither have I heard tell of aught built in pagan times that could rival in grace this Dome of the Rock.' The Dome of the Rock itself was set up also, however, 'to stand comparison with the great Church of the Christians' (as one manuscript of al-Muqaddasi bluntly states about the al-Aqsa; he is almost certainly referring to the Church of the Holy Sepulchre). It was a gesture of religious politics. It is even suggested, particularly by enemies of Abd al-Malik's Umayyad dynasty, that it was asserting the authority of this region over and against Mecca – a political gesture in the internal civil wars of the early history of Islam. The position and magnificence of the construction of the building certainly make a stunning statement. It was a building that proclaimed the mission of Islam as much as it commemorated and transcended the religious history embodied in the Temple Mount.

The building's octagonal shape shows a strong influence of Byzantine architecture (it led one nineteenth-century British archaeologist, in what is a familiar imperialist strategy, to claim stridently that the Dome was actually built by Constantine and was originally a Christian monument. The marble itself almost certainly did come from earlier Christian or pagan buildings). It is inscribed with verses from the Qur'an, the first evidence of a written text for this scripture, which also form part of Suleiman's decorations (Figure 19). The glimmering cupola, which so dominates the skyline of Jerusalem, is about 20 metres in diameter and stands some 30 metres high (and has been repeatedly repaired over the centuries). This central cylinder is built closely around the rock itself, which determines its scale (Figure 20). The cupola is supported by a circular arcade of four piers and twelve columns. Around that, there is an octagonal arcade of eight piers and sixteen columns. Between the circular and octagonal arcade, there is a richly decorated ambulatory, as there is between the octagonal arcade and the octagonal outer walls.

19. The highly ornate tiles added to the Dome of the Rock by Suleiman the Magnificent. As well as the intricate abstract patterns, there is a calligraphic inscription of verses from the Qur'an.

20. The rock inside the Dome of the Rock. Through the pillars and piers
which surround it, you can see the lavishly decorated ambulatories
(walkways) which circle the bare rock.

The rock is thus framed at the centre of ambulatories, created by sets of pillars and piers. The whole building has a diameter of about 48 metres and the ambulatories are only about 11 metres in height. Like the Temple of Solomon, this is a building which does not rely on size for its impressive effect.

The arcades of columns and piers are decorated with mosaics of elaborate abstract design in gold, red, blue and turquoise. Stained glass windows give a softly mottled light. The ceilings of the ambulatories have large gilded panels in the form of rosettes and interlacing star patterns. These were almost entirely redone in the 1960s, imitating patterns created in the thirteenth century. (Much of the decoration has been extensively renovated and even redesigned over the years, up to and including the late twentieth century.) The piers are faced with single, split-faced and quartered panels of marble and stone. The whole effect of glittering splendour in shaded light is overwhelming, especially in contrast to the simple rock at its centre.

This building has become *the* icon of Jerusalem – and as such is unviewable without the swaddling clothes of history. Its very visibility has made it the perfect symbol to fight and long for.

BOILING AND GRILLING PAGANS

The First Crusade brought the violent force of Christianity back to Jerusalem. In 1095 Pope Urban II launched an army to conquer the infidels in the Holy Land. In 1099, Jerusalem was taken. The sack of the city was brutal. The romance of the Middle Ages thrilled Victorian Britain, and the Crusaders, especially Richard the Lionheart, appear all too often as chivalrous knights on a holy mission. The entrance into Jerusalem, however, was horrific in its indiscriminate murder. Despite the surrender of the Muslim commander and promises given, the Crusaders slaughtered everyone they could lay their hands on. They burnt buildings full of people. When Raymond of Aguilers, a Crusader leader, visited the Temple area, he had to walk over so many corpses that the blood reached up to his knees. This was not a solitary example of grotesque bloodthirstiness. Radulph of Caen describes how on the campaign 'our troops boiled pagan adults in cooking pots; they impaled children on spits and consumed them grilled'. Cannibalism is a standard insult of the enemy; it is a less common accusation of one's own troops. The soldiers of Christendom banned non-Christians from Jerusalem and began their military rule over the area.

The Dome of the Rock was renamed Templum Domini, the Temple of Our Lord, and in a simple but potent display of triumph, a cross was placed at the top of the Dome. It is a strange quirk of history that this Islamic shrine then became the dominant image of the Jewish Temple for Western Christians. Figure 21 is exemplary. It shows Raphael's lovely *Marriage of the Virgin*, now in Milan. The impressive back-drop, which draws the eye away from the marriage ceremony to the theologically charged edifice of the Temple, is an Italianate version of the Dome. That's how the Temple looked to Raphael and his audience. The image of the Temple is constantly being re-created in this way out of a mixture of history, politics, visual tradition and imagination.

The other buildings on the Temple Mount were also taken over and adapted for the Crusaders' use. The al-Aqsa Mosque became the headquarters of the newly formed order

21. Raphael's *Marriage of the Virgin* (now in the Brera, Milan), with its image of the temple based on the Dome of the Rock.

of the Knights Templar (who will reappear in chapter 11). They called the Mosque the Templum Solomonis, Temple of Solomon, because they believed that this was the site of the first Temple. They also stabled their horses in the under-ground vaults at the south-eastern section of the Temple Mount platform, which they called Solomon's Stables. New rituals were invented. The eastern gate, known as the Golden Gate, was walled up. In Jewish *midrashic* tradition, the Messiah will enter through this gate, and Christians believed that Jesus entered through it on Palm Sunday. Perhaps because of such stories, the door was blocked off after Omar's conquest of Jerusalem. The Crusaders, however, opened it twice a year, once on Palm Sunday and once on a new feast celebrating the arrival in Jerusalem of the True Cross, which the Byzantine emperor Heraclius was said to have recovered from the Persians. The Temple Mount, so long left empty as a sign of the triumph of Christianity, now glittered with buildings and rituals which celebrated that self-same triumph. A physical Christian Temple stood over Jerusalem.

The Christian rule did not last even a century, however, although it had a profound influence on Western memory and a huge number of buildings erected during this period still stand, including a large part of the old city of Jerusalem. The great general Saladin led a Muslim army to recover Jerusalem, and to replace the cross with a crescent. Just as the destruction of the second Temple by Titus is said to have taken place on the same day in the calendar as the destruc-tion of the first Temple by Nebuchadnezzar (9 Av), so the retaking of Jerusalem on 2 October 1187 is said to be the same day in the Muslim calendar (27 Rajab) as that on which Mohammed ascended to heaven from Jerusalem. In the history of the Temple there are no coincidences, only narratives fraught with symbolic significance. It was only with the Crusades that the contest over the Temple itself became a fully symbolic struggle between East and West. After the Crusades, any struggle over the Temple falls all too easily into a rhetorical pattern. It's either Western assault and Saladin-like heroic defence of Islamic values, or it's the salvation of Western culture from the barbarian. With the Temple it is impossible, it seems, to escape the burden of history.

8

....

THE ARTIST'S EYE

Raphael's image of the Temple is a telling example of how architectural realities can feed into the artistic tradition in surprising ways. But the majority of artists who worked to produce images of the Temple relied on written sources and each other's work. This has produced a wonderful repertoire of representations of the Temple, from drawings to paintings to grand models for exhibition. These portrayals inevitably reveal as much about the culture of the time of their production as they do about the ancient world. But they also feed back into later written discussions and future pictures, as the tradition of thinking about the Temple develops.

From the seventeenth to the nineteenth centuries, the bare description of Solomon's Temple from the Bible is fleshed out by archaeological science and architectural training, and a rich set of images is produced, where the artist's imagination and cultural milieu deeply influence the pursuit of historical truth. There are many hundreds of images of Solomon's Temple produced from the Renaissance onwards that show this self-revealing process of creative reconstruction. I have chosen a few examples here of pictures and models from the Renaissance up to today which capture this artistic tradition especially nicely.

Juan Bautista Villalpando was a Spanish Jesuit who,

together with Hieronymo Prado, published a three-volume treatise between 1594 and 1605 on the vision of Ezekiel. It proved highly influential on later illustrators. Figure 22 shows superbly how much Villalpando absorbed from the Renaissance architecture of royal palaces and its classicism. This notion of Solomon's Temple looks glaringly anachronistic to modern eyes. The building follows the principles of the Roman architect Vitruvius (as neo-classical architects should), and revels in symmetries of form and balance of proportions (as well as having a lot of windows for a building said in the Bible to be no more than fifty metres long!). The need for grandeur of a particular aristocratic and scholarly sort has quite overtaken any commitment to historical accuracy.

Bernard Lamy, a French priest with a passion for mathematics and philosophy, showed little respect for Villalpando's lack of historical sense. He returned with a sense of purpose to the texts themselves, especially the Book of Chronicles, and produced an architectural plan for a square, pillared temple, with a 120-cubit-high tower. But he was also fascinated by the architecture of the platform of the Temple Mount and his monumental book *De Tabernaculo Foederis, de sancta Civitate Jerusalem et de Templo eius* (*On the Ark of the Covenant, the Holy City of Jerusalem and Its Temple*), published posthumously in 1720, contains an astounding representation of the substructure of the platform (Figure 23). This image, which reveals Lamy's love of mathematical structures, looks more like an Escher print from the heyday of German expressionism than an Enlightenment study. Lamy's austere return to the biblical texts did not prevent him from the most expansive flights of fancy.

VNIVERSI TEMPLI HIEROSOLYMITANI ORTHOGRAPHIA QVAE OSTENDIT ORIENTALEM FACIEM

22. The elevation of the temple, as imagined by Juan Bautista Villalpando,
In Ezechielem Explanationes (1594–1603): a masterpiece of
Renaissance palace architecture.

RI ATRII EXTERIORIS ET PARTEM MVRI PORTICVS GENTIVM QVAE DEINDE DICTA EST SALOMONI

23. The substructure of Solomon's Temple as imagined by Bernard Lamy in his *de Tabernaculo* (1720).

Conrad Schick was a German architect and missionary who settled in Jerusalem in the later part of the nineteenth century. He helped found and design Mea Shearim, which is now the ultra-orthodox section of the city. He spent fifty years investigating the archaeology of Jerusalem, and he was renowned for constructing large-scale wooden models of the city and its monuments. He built a model of the Tabernacle, which was visited in Jerusalem by the Prussian crown prince and the Austrian emperor, before successfully touring the British Isles ('bringing the Holy Land to those who cannot visit it': the exhibition was counted a great success by his missionary employers). After it was exhibited at the 1873 World's Fair at Vienna, his model of the Holy Sepulchre was bought by the king of Württemberg, who rewarded him with a knighthood. He was also commissioned by the Sultan of the Ottoman Empire for a model of the Temple Mount for the same exhibition, as he wrote proudly to Captain Wilson, of Wilson's Arch renown (which other archaeologists hoped vainly would open access to hitherto forbidden areas). But the crowning glory of his career was a further model of the Temple Mount in four sections, each of which represented a different period. It could be taken apart and put together to show the topography of the site, Solomon's Temple, the destruction and reconstruction by Zerubbabel and Herod, and finally the Muslim Haram al-Sharif. It was built in 1885 and exhibited posthumously at the World's Fair at St Louis in 1904, where it was sold for the huge sum of £800.

Figure 24 shows the model in the epoch of Solomon's Temple. For all his archaeological research – he did some sterling work on the underground cisterns of the Temple Mount and had the reputation of being his generation's most learned scholar of the physical city – this model of Solomon's compound is deeply imbued with a classical tradition. Its columned porticos and symmetrical, well-proportioned buildings reveal the training of a nineteenth-century architect. His drawing of the façade of Solomon's Temple, however, looks somewhat different. It is flamboyantly ornate, with more than a touch of Grand Vienna (Figure 25). Its fussy balustrades and decorated cornices, the windows with their orientalising frames (sitting awkwardly above classical swags) evoke an Easternised vision of European cathedral architecture. For Schick, working for the Western audience typified by the crowds at the World's Fair, this is what Solomon's Temple needed to look like.

This process of creative reconstruction is no less evident with Herod's Temple, where the detailed verbal descriptions and measurements provided by Josephus (a classical source) and the Bible and Talmud (an even more authoritative source for generations of religious scholars) provide a matrix of limitations different from the descriptions of Solomon's buildings. This makes the wild variations all the more telling. Figure 26 is Schick's again, and it shows remarkable similarities to his reconstruction of the façade of Solomon's Temple (Figure 25). The ideological lure of continuity is strongly marked here. It is as if Herod's claim to rebuild the second Temple according to the scale and plans of the first is fully instantiated in the same baroque windows, multi-levelled porticos and triangular towers. The dimensions are carefully inscribed on the drawing to make plain the equivalence. For the missionary archaeologist, the recognisable continuity of the first and second Temples is the grounding of a religious and cultural history.

James Fergusson was an expert in art and archaeology at the centre of the British establishment, a Victorian gentleman and scholar, who was a massively influential figure, particularly in the study of Indian art and architecture in Britain. A Scot, he was educated at Edinburgh High School, but did not go to university; he had made a substantial fortune, however, by the age of 25 with an indigo factory in India, and retired to London, from where he travelled, studied and wrote. It was he who proposed that the Dome of the Rock was originally really a Christian building built by Constantine. ('No one saw the facts in the same light in which I saw them, and the conclusion which I had drawn from them was consequently looked upon as an idle dream, and their author was treated with scant courtesy.') He wrote extensively about the archaeology of the Middle and Far East, including many fine drawings of distant places for the armchair traveller to enjoy. His reconstruction of Herod's Temple, which, like Schick's, claims to be based on an exhaustive examination of the ancient evidence, fits very comfortably into this sequence of illustrations from abroad (Figure 27).

He is not impressed by Solomon's or Herod's ground-plan. 'A building 100 cubits wide, 100 cubits high, 100 cubits long, is necessarily stumpy, and deficient in poetry of proportion,' he declares, and his drawing is designed to do his best with such recalcitrant facts, and the angle of the view is chosen to minimise the ugliness of the offensive four-square plan. But unlike Schick, Fergusson did not see the history of the Temple as one of continuity, but rather one that fitted into the most up-to-date Victorian notions of progress: 'It would be difficult in the whole range of architectural history

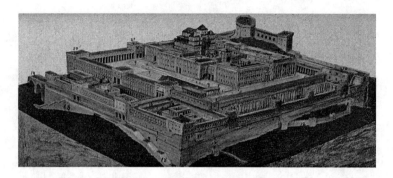

24. The model of Solomon's Temple, pictured from the south-east, and made by Conrad Schick in the late-nineteenth century.

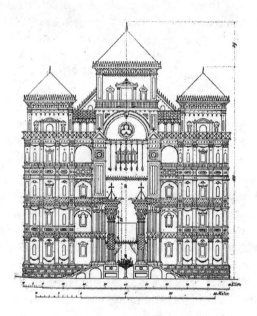

25. The front of Solomon's Temple as pictured by Conrad Schick (1896).

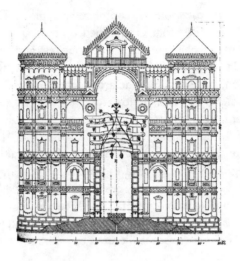

26. The front of Herod's Temple as pictured by Conrad Schick (1896).

27. Herod's Temple as pictured by James Fergusson (1878).

[133]

to find a more curious or complete example of Darwinian development than that exemplified by the various changes the Temple of the Jews underwent when restored or rebuilt at various intervals during the long period of its existence.' For Fergusson, the Temple is the architectural equivalent of the development of Judaism towards the modern religion of Christianity. It's a building on the move. What culminated in Herod's Temple began with the Tabernacle in the desert. Fergusson offered a picture of this too (Figure 28). Despite the hangings visible behind the supporting pillars, and the carefully Oriental figures for scale, this Tabernacle looks like nothing so much as a Victorian army tent, perhaps one from the British Empire in India, where Fergusson had worked at length. His Darwinism is pictured in wonderfully Victorian colours.

It is well worth comparing the drawings of the Victorians Fergusson and Schick with a later drawing, also by a distinguished archaeologist. Carl Watzinger was Professor of Archaeology at Tübingen, one of Germany's leading institutions, from 1916 until his death in 1948 – the dates, of course, are significant: he held his position throughout the Nazi era. He was most famous for his excavation of Jericho, and he was a celebrated pioneer of modern archaeology in sites all over the Middle East. Between 1933 and 1935 he published his two-volume *Denkmäler Palästinas* (*Monuments of Palestine*). It need hardly be emphasised that the Nazi ideology of Aryanism (coupled with long-held racist beliefs) made Palestine and the Jewish roots of Christianity a charged subject in the German academy in particular at this time. German architecture too, with its long debt to classicism, was entering a new period of monumental design, led by the

28. The Tabernacle of Moses in the desert, as imagined by
James Fergusson (1878).

state-sponsored building programme. This must change the way we now see Watzinger's version of the Temple of Herod (Figure 29). Unlike the reconstructions of Schick or Fergusson, this is austere and classical, a simple four-square design around classically proportioned columns. The only element of decoration allowed is an eagle set over the doorway.

Watzinger knew his Josephus well. According to the Jewish historian, Herod placed an eagle over the doorway of the Temple as a sign of his allegiance to Rome. The eagle topped Roman standards, which were carried into battle, and was the distinctive symbol of the Roman state. But Josephus also tells us that the eagle caused a storm of protest from the inhabitants of Jerusalem and had to be taken down. (As with the cross and the crescent of later centuries, it really matters under whose banner the Temple stands.) Watzinger is depicting the Temple no doubt on the day of its dedication, the architect's original design rather than how it stood after the compromise with popular taste. But it is hard to forget that the word fascism comes from the *fasces*, bunches of sticks which were carried as signs of authority by officials in ancient Rome, and that the eagle was adopted by the Nazi state as its distinctive symbol also. This drawing of Watzinger's is indeed the only example I have seen in the many hundreds of reconstructions of Herod's Temple to include the eagle, let alone to take it as the only element of decoration. Watzinger's Temple could have been designed by Albert Speer.

29. The front of Herod's Temple, as pictured by the German archaeologist,
Carl Watzinger in 1933.

Conrad Schick's models were famous, but he was not the only person to produce models of Jerusalem or of the Temple compound. There was in fact a long tradition of making models – often for educational purposes, but also out of artistic or religious zeal. These days, most are concealed in out-of-the-way religious institutions or museum basements, but they reveal a forgotten history of how the Temple enters the popular imagination. One remarkable figure in this history is Jacob Judah Leon, known as Leon Templo because of his famous model of the Temple. He was a Dutch Jew of the late seventeenth century who came to London, where he was the first Jew to receive a royal warrant and the first Jew to compose a prayer for the king – the 'Royal Prayer' – for use in synagogues. His model of the Temple was massive: in the advertising, it was boasted that it was 20 feet by 10 feet by 7 feet in size. It was exhibited in Amsterdam first, where it was seen by King Charles II and his entourage. This led to his trip to England, where the model became a fashionable and popular wonder to visit. The advertisement posters still survive: you could make a visit and buy books between 9 o'clock and 11, and again between 2 o'clock and 5. Explanatory descriptions of the model were printed in eight languages.

Leon Templo was an enlightened and educated man. He was sent to Sir Christopher Wren with a letter of introduction as a man whose intention was 'to shew in England a curious model of the Temple of Salaomon … where he doth presume to have demonstrated and corrected an infinite number of errors and paralogismes of our most learned scholars, who have meddled with the exposition of that holy fabrick, and most specially of the Jesuit Villalpandus'. His

30. Jacob Judah Leon *Retrato del Templo de Selomoh* (Middleburg, 1640): a view of Solomon's Temple, his palace and Fortress Antonia. Leon's model was the first to utilize Talmudic sources.

model does not survive, but the published drawings are certainly a startling corrective of Villalpando's aristocratic neoclassical palace. Leon Templo's building is perched on a huge platform. The walls of the platform are supported by massive buttresses, and immense stairways can be seen on either side leading up to the upper level from Solomon's Palace and, anachronistically, from the Antonia fortress. The Temple is placed asymmetrically to the north-east of the platform, as the biblical sources suggest, and it is a simple, somewhat squat building of three storeys (as Fergusson feared), a building quite without the embellishments of Victorian imagination, or the classical expansions of Villalpando. The models of Templo reached a broad audience, and his books were widely translated through Europe. (They didn't stop Gerhard Schott, a German Christian, from making a full-scale wood model in 1695, based slavishly on Villalpando's drawings, a model which can be seen today in Hamburg.) But Templo was influential, not only because he brought Talmudic discussions into his ideas of reconstruction, but also because he had an impact on a group beginning to rise in public awareness in London: the Freemasons. This strange turn of Templo's career, however, will have to wait until chapter 11.

Where drawings encourage the wonder of visualisation, the three-dimensional model encourages a different physical response. Models are to be walked round, to touch, to feel oneself entering. They are designed to help place the viewer in a landscape, a landscape of the miraculous past. The doll's house encourages different play from a book. This helps explain the continuing attraction of models of the Temple. Perhaps none is odder, or more weirdly impressive, than the

31. Alec Garrard's model, a close up of the colonnade on the Temple Mount.

work of the Suffolk farmer Alec Garrard, who over thirty years has been building a scale model of the Temple in one of his barns (Figure 31). 'People say I am inspired by God,' he told me in his East Anglian drawl, 'but I am not.' The measurements and the reconstruction are regarded as so accurate that scholar after scholar – Alec refers to them familiarly by their first names – has traipsed across the farmyard to visit him and discuss his sometimes rather novel theories. When I visited, the model had been temporarily moved to Bullock Fair Charity Centre in the village of Harleston, where it was available to be seen on Sundays, an image of the Holy Land for rural Norfolk. England's green and pleasant fields have their rebuilt Jerusalem after all.

'Let them measure the pattern': rebuilding the Temple in art and as a model shows most clearly how the Temple is a monument of the imagination. Different cultural periods and obsessions produce very different images of the building. The lost Temple has to be pictured, but *how* it is pictured is hugely revealing both of the artist and of his cultural expectations and hopes. How the Temple is rebuilt in the mind is an expression of the hopes and dreams of the age.

9

....

TRAVELLERS' TALES

'AS IF THE PAST WERE MORE TRULY BEFORE ME'

Schick's model brought the Holy Land to those who could not visit it. But from the moment David, leaping and dancing, brought the Ark to the city, pilgrimage to Jerusalem has been a constant demand. While the Temple stood, the pilgrim festivals brought Jews to their religious centre; after the destruction, even when Jews were banned, a few were allowed to return once a year to mourn the destruction. It was this occasion that provoked St Jerome's pitiless scorn, a reaction imitated by many others in later years. Christians began to travel to the sites of the life of Jesus, and then to those of the saints, from the earliest times. 'How is it possible to pass through places full of Passion without passion?' asks Gregory of Nyssa. To go on pilgrimage is to pursue the religious fervour enacted in those places at that time. The Temple Dome is a place of pilgrimage for Muslims rather than a mosque – the opportunity to see where Mohammed ascended. For the religious pilgrim, to travel to the site of the Temple is to make a journey towards what is lost, a past that still burns with significance in the present.

The difficulty of travel, war between the Ottoman Empire and the West, and the dangers of the road meant that travel to Jerusalem from Western Europe was a serious and often religiously motivated activity that few were prepared to undertake before the eighteenth century. But from the days of the Grand Tour onwards, not only did more and more people make the journey, but also they wrote about it at greater length and from a great range of perspectives. The latest bibliography of 'travellers' tales' to Palestine lists over 12,000 entries for the years 1878–95 alone. Western travellers came to Jerusalem to enter the world of the Bible, which played such a formative role in their minds, and they came to see the sites whose names had such an evocative history. They also came to record their impressions for a public at home. What they saw was a place where the Temple had once stood, and a Middle Eastern city of small houses and narrow streets. Caught between the Romantic lure of the history in the stones and their own disappointment at how Jerusalem could never fully match the glories of the biblical past in their imaginations, the nineteenth-century travellers wrote to explore that bittersweet experience.

'The Itinerary of a Certain Englishman' (1344–5), one of our earliest accounts of a trip to Jerusalem, has few anxieties. The anonymous pilgrim visited the Temple Mount ('a very large place, like an estate, a very white one, as if it were covered in snow') and wrote baldly of the Dome of the Rock, 'In that house were the Ark, the Propitiatory, the Golden Candlesticks and the other figurative things which are written.' For him, the Dome is the Temple of the Lord and so it is where the holy objects had been placed. Typical of the nineteenth-century traveller, however, is Robert Richardson, who published his *Travels along the Mediterranean and Parts Adjacent* in 1822. 'These plain embattled walls in the midst of a barren mountain track, do they enclose the city of

Jerusalem?' he wondered as he approached the city. 'Where was the Temple of Solomon, and where is Mount Zion, the glory of the whole earth?' For Richardson, what is to be seen at Jerusalem is always a question. It is the traveller's emotions and thoughts, as much as the site itself, which need exploring.

Richardson was a doctor who was travelling with the illustrious Countess of Belmore, and as they tour the city, including a trip to the Temple Mount thanks to the invitation and protection of Omar Effendi, his reactions become more complex than his initial hesitations. 'Come now,' he invites the reader, 'and see the City of the Prophets and Apostles, walk round the walls of Jerusalem, and consider the woes of Mount Zion.' His patron the Countess is introduced as the perfect traveller: she 'visited the memorable spots in and about Jerusalem with all the zeal and feeling of a pious Christian, taking the Holy Scriptures as her guide'. That is the ideal way to be a visitor to the holy city: as a pilgrim, with the Bible in hand, and not as a tourist with a Baedeker. As Richardson notes, 'It is impossible for the Christian traveller to look upon Jerusalem with the same feelings with which he would set himself to contemplate the ruins of Thebes, of Athens or of Rome.' This sentence reveals two basic expectations of the Victorian traveller. First, the explicit or implicit point of comparison is always the glory that was Greece and the grandeur that was Rome: the Grand Tour was primarily to the classical sites of Italy, and the classical ruins set the standard for the sublime power of ancient buildings over the imagination. Second, a traveller does not just visit such a place. He must 'set himself to contemplate'. He must stop, observe, reflect and ruminate on the past. Unlike the flitting tourist, the traveller's thoughts are profound and considered and worth publishing in a book.

When Richardson visits the Temple Mount, despite his earlier reactions, he is deeply impressed, 'It seems as if the glory of the temple still dwelt upon the mosque and the glory of Solomon still covered the site of his temple.' He also is clear from his scientific reading of the Bible that the Dome could not be the site of the Holy of Holies if the al-Aqsa Mosque is the site of Solomon's Temple, as his guide claimed. The measurements do not fit. The archetypal Victorian traveller is well armed with a scholarly appreciation of the Bible, and he needs to show his authoritative understanding. This is less pressing for a woman, for whom piety is a greater calling in Victorian public life. So with an insouciance that may seem surprising for a pilgrim, Frederika Bremer in *Travels in the Holy Land* (translated from the German into English in 1862) reaches for higher feelings: 'Whether it were exactly here or there is of little consequence to the spiritual mind.' Bremer's book displays her 'spiritual mind' as much as the sites of Jerusalem.

Yet for Richardson, as for most travellers, articulating a response to Jerusalem's holy sites also meant expressing one's own religious commitments. Richardson sets a tone that many British travellers adopted when faced by the competing groups of monks and clerics. He despises their worldliness and aggression, and describes in epic sarcasm a fight between the Roman Catholic and the Greek Orthodox monks: 'we witnessed all the tug of war, the biting and the scratching, the pommeling and the pelting, the brickbats and the clubs, the whimpering and the mewling, of ecstatic, squawling, palpitating monks fighting for their chapel, like kites or crows for their nest'. He registers his disgust at a priest he saw at the Holy Sepulchre: 'a greasy rotundity of frame and a puffed up aspect of pride, full of war and contention'. For the Protestant, it is no surprise that the Muslims call *these* Christians 'dogs and idolators'.

But Richardson is also fascinated by the continuing presence of Jews in Jerusalem: 'I should look at the ceremonies of Pagan temples as a matter of little more than idle curiosity: but the ceremonies of the Jews dip into the heart.' The Jews allow Richardson to reach back through history: 'I never see the fine venerable aspect of a Jew but I feel for him as an elder brother.'

While Richardson can feel his way back towards the Temple by his contact with the Jews and their religious life, others are less warm. Charles Warren, the archaeologist and soldier whom we will meet in the next chapter, describes with distaste Western visitors to the Wailing Wall 'who walked about laughing and making remarks, as though it were all a farce'. But Richardson also finds Jewish women very attractive in a somewhat less spiritual way: 'admirers of size and softness in the fair sex will find as regularly well-built fatties, with double mouldings in the neck and chin, among the fair daughters of Jerusalem as among the fairer daughters of England'. Not exactly modern terms of praise (though this is the first use in English of the noun 'fatty'), but time and again Victorian travellers talk at length about the Jews of Jerusalem as a way of trying to express their feelings for the religious past – and time and again add comments about the beauty of Jewish women. It is in this context that descriptions, drawing and photographs of Jews at the Wailing Wall become a commonplace.

While comments on the beauty of the foreign women, like comments on the character of the cowardly and untrustworthy Muslims, are all too recognisable reactions of the British imperial gentleman viewing the Oriental Other, it must not be forgotten that these travellers' tales are also ways in which Christian visitors strove to articulate their reactions to the religious power of the city and Temple of Jerusalem. Coming into contact with Jews here in Jerusalem, in a way they may not have done in London or Paris, provoked and sharpened the Christian's sense of what a trip to the historical site of the Temple might mean. These vignettes of Jews or Muslims in Jerusalem are mirrors in which Christians saw how history mattered to them.

Harriet Martineau was one of the most important and widely read female authors of the nineteenth century. She retired to her bed in the Lake District twenty years before her death in 1876, from where she published books, articles and an autobiography that made her a lionised literary celebrity and the *grande dame* of Victorian middle-class feminism. Her three-volume *Eastern Life: Present and Past* (1848) is based on an eight-month trip to the Middle East. Martineau was fully part of the intellectual ferment around Christianity and science in Victorian Britain. In the wonderfully titled 'How to Observe Manners and Morals', an essay on how to be a foreigner abroad, she fully welcomes the geological and biological discoveries that were so threatening to Victorian understandings of the truth of the Bible. One should know about 'vast spaces of time' and the 'huge revolutions of nature', she advises the traveller. None the less, *Eastern Life* is also a self-aware and entertaining defence of middle-of-the-road Christian views at a time of crisis in the church. Like Richardson, she dislikes 'grovelling superstition' and mere 'formal observance'; like Richardson, she finds the Jews 'a very handsome race, with eyes that seem to distinguish them from the rest of mankind – large, soft and of the deepest expression'. But Martineau is most concerned to explore what history means in such a place for her and others like her. She distinguishes between the history of a religion and its true value: we must avoid 'the awful error of mistaking the Records of the origin of Judaism and Christianity for the messages themselves'. For Martineau, Christianity is developing in a Darwinian way, improving slowly but surely. But it is by the Temple that she feels the real pull of the 'vast spaces of time':

> *But with all this before my eyes, my mind was with the past. It seemed as if the past were more truly before me than what I saw. Here was the ground chosen by David, and levelled by Solomon to receive the Temple.*

This leads to two pages of emotive description of 'these places [which] had been so familiar to my mind's eye from my youth up'. Martineau carefully anatomises her own response. The space was familiar from her reading, but when she sees the site of the Temple, her mind is drawn beyond the signs of the past, the ruins, into a sense of the past itself: as if she were there. This is the classic statement of the yearning of the traveller to see – to experience – the Temple.

AN OLD ETONIAN CLUB

It is against such emotional accounts that one of the funniest and most popular travel books of the nineteenth century was written: A.W. Kinglake's *Eothen*. Kinglake was an Old Etonian who cultivated the narrative voice of an intelligent but fey man-about-town, who always wishes to appear effortlessly in control and amusedly detached. The title of his book means 'From the East' in ancient Greek (which sets the tone of refined cultivation). He wittily dissects the conventions of the traveller's tale: 'there are people who can visit an interesting locality, and follow up continuously the exact train of thought that ought to be suggested by the historical associations of the place ... I am not thus docile: it is only by snatches, and for a few moments together, that I can really associate a place with its proper history.' Where Richardson and Martineau muse on the beauty of the Jews, Kinglake advises on how to make contact with the Christian girls of Bethlehem: 'If you will only look virtuous enough to prevent alarm, and vicious enough to avoid looking silly, the blithe maidens will draw nearer and nearer to you.' Where Martineau worries earnestly about the etiquette of other countries, Kinglake calmly bridges the gap: 'The love of tea is a glad sense of fellow feeling between the Englishman and the Asiatic.' He is also gently mocking of the visitor who walks with Bible in hand: there are, he notes, 'many geographical surprises that puzzle the "Bible Christian"'. But most of all, he revels in the humorous mismatch of the London man-about-town at sea in the world of Jerusalem. 'It will seem almost strange to you to find yourself so entirely surrounded in all your daily doings by the signs and sounds of religion. Your hotel is a monastery ... Your club is the great Church of the Holy Sepulchre.' His mock bafflement at finding religion in Jerusalem takes an irreverent sideswipe at the host of pilgrims and their journeying to find their place in religious history at the site of the Temple.

Everyone approaches the Temple with preconceptions, and for Western Europeans over the centuries these preconceptions have been formed not only by the Bible or other ancient sources, but also by the flood of travellers' descriptions. Particularly in the nineteenth century, when institutional Christianity was struggling against the growing authority of science and a new sense of history that comes from Darwinism and from geology, Christian travellers to Jerusalem found themselves inevitably mired in a heightened and conflicted sense of the past, and wrote about it again and again. What was there to see and feel at the site of the Temple, this most charged of absent monuments? Encountering Jews, Muslims and different types of Christianity, how was the Western Christian to 'set himself to contemplate' the past and the commitments of present day? The Temple became a space to investigate one's place in history. What the traveller saw in the empty mirror of the Temple was his own self.

ARCHAEOLOGY AND IMPERIALISM

JERUSALEM WARREN

The Renaissance made classical architecture and sculpture the dominant model for building and for the plastic arts in Western Europe. The Grand Tour brought the ideals of classical form back from Italy and, occasionally, from Greece; sculptures were discovered, bought and looted, and consequently transported home to private houses and then to museums. This development changed the face of the public buildings of Europe and the mental landscape of the artistic imagination. In the hands of Michelangelo, David now appears like a young Greek hero. Archaeology is one of the master disciplines of the Renaissance: the desire of the Renaissance to make the classical past shine again required the archaeologists' brilliant discoveries. They uncovered the lost buildings and the works of art to excite their contemporaries' fascination with ancient Greece and Rome. The unprecedented unearthing in the eighteenth century of the town of Pompeii, apparently frozen in lava since the first century, further heightened the glamour of archaeology. When Heinrich Schliemann in the nineteenth century announced to the world 'Today I have looked on the face of Agamemnon', and when he declared that he had uncovered the city of Troy, it was the fulfilment of an age's passion. In

Egypt too, the gradually revealed secrets of the Pyramids and the discovery of the tomb of Tutankhamun, made an international story of lasting interest. In Crete, the discovery of the palace of Knossos in the early twentieth century seemed to create a world for the Greek myths of the labyrinth and the Minotaur. Archaeology was a sexy subject well before Indiana Jones.

Against such a background it is astonishing that there has been so little archaeology in and around the Temple. As we saw, Jericho was excavated by Conrad Schick, Dura-Europos offered its decorated synagogue, and numerous other temple sites in the Middle East have been explored, along with a host of public and private buildings. But there have been only two significant excavations near the Temple Mount, both of which were the source of heated controversy, and there has been no excavation at all on the Mount itself. The reason for the absence of digging on the Temple Mount is simple: the Waqf, the Muslim authorities, resolutely refuse to allow it, and the orthodox Jewish community is also firmly opposed. This is a sacred place and not to be disturbed. This makes the politics of digging in Jerusalem fantastically complex, and the stories of both Captain Warren's dig in the 1870s and Professor Mazar's, which finished in the 1970s make for riveting reading. A hundred years is a long time in politics, but the two stories together tell us a great deal about the connection between archaeology and imperialism, and archaeology and vested interests.

The Palestine Exploration Fund was a committee set up in 1863. Its foundation was partly due to a benefaction by Miss Burdett Coutts to improve the water supply to Jerusalem. Within a year it was manned by a group of powerful Victorian grandees who wished to 'throw light on some of the problems of Biblical History, and of the topography of ancient sites in the Holy city'. This was one of the very influential private committees and clubs that were so important to the Victorian system. It included the Archbishop of Canterbury, the Duke of Argyll, the Earl of Shaftesbury, Dr Pusey, Sir Henry Rawlinson, George Grove (the head of the Royal College of Music) and Sir Walter Besant (novelist and antiquarian) – a who's who of the great and the good in the world of religion and the arts. In 1867 they appointed Captain Warren of the Royal Engineers, with three corporals, to complete the survey work started by Captain Wilson (who gave his name to Wilson's Arch). Warren turned out to be an inspired choice, and this project was the first step in a career which would lead him to fight in some of the most famous battles of the Boer War, including the relief of Ladysmith, to be appointed as head of the Metropolitan Police in London and to retire as a famous national figure, General Sir Charles Warren GCMG, KCB, FRS.

Warren was a true *Boy's Own* hero of the British Empire. There are only two books a youth needs, he declared, the Bible and Baden-Powell's *Scouting for Boys*. He set off, according to his biographer and grandson, 'somewhat in the *rôle* of a Crusader ... for he was stirred by the longing to reveal to the Christian world those Sacred Places which were hidden by the *débris* of many a siege and jealously guarded by the Turkish Mussulmans'. When blocked by the Turkish authorities, he reflected, 'I had two courses before me – either to effect my object by stealth or else go straightforward and see if the perseverance of an Englishman would not at last overpower opposition.' In the end he

32. General Sir Charles Warren.

resorted to both strategies. His perseverance took the form of blunt diplomacy, an upright public honesty that refused to compromise on any issue, and a deep disdain for Turkish manners and customs. His stealth was equally necessary. He was eventually allowed to dig some way away from the walls, so he dug down, and then, underground, opened another trench at right-angles to the first until he reached his goal. Blithely ignoring religious sensitivities, he secretly entered the holiest sites of Islam at night, and when the bribed guards became nervous he dismissively commented: 'All these people are like children; if they think over the prospect of anything dangerous, they get frightened and slink out of it.' Modern accounts of Warren's excavations always call him 'intrepid' and 'heroic' – in the grand tradition of muscular archaeology. There is very little reflection on the imperialist attitudes that made his work possible.

None the less, the excavations did change everyone's understanding of the topography of the Temple area, and did require a good deal of physical bravery. It was Warren who uncovered and explored the underground passages which are essential to the water supply of the district (and which are now part of every visitor's trip to the area of the Temple Mount). His survey revealed numerous new understandings of the general geographical features of the area. In short, as he puts it with customary directness, 'I have put the whole subject of the topography on a new footing.'

His description of how he traced the course of one passage shows why he is so often called 'intrepid'. It was a magnificent tunnel, 10 metres high, carved into the rock. But it was full of 'sewage [which] was not water, and was not mud'. He and his faithful assistant Corporal Birtles brought three doors to spread their weight. With nervous balance, they stood each on one door and passed the third along; they made slow progress for several hundred feet. The passage was getting narrower and narrower, and conditions were perilous. 'Everything had now become so slippery with sewage that we had to exercise the greatest caution in lowering the doors and ourselves down, lest an unlucky false step might cause a header into the murky liquid – a fall which must have been fatal – and what honour would there have been in dying like a rat in a pool of sewage?' Eventually, they heard voices and feet and realised they were directly below the palace (*serai*) of the Pacha. It is easy to see why the London newspapers sent out reporters and artists to record the adventures of 'Jerusalem Warren'.

Warren fully repaid the trust of the Palestine Exploration Fund. As Sir Walter Besant wrote:

> *It was Warren ... who stripped the rubbish from the rocks, and showed the glorious Temple standing within its walls, 1,000 feet long and 200 feet high, of mighty masonry; he it was who laid open the valleys now covered up and hidden; he who opened the secret passages, the ancient aqueducts, the bridge connecting the Temple to the town.*

In this encomium, the archaeologist is the hero who removes the dirt to reveal the truth, who uncovers the secrets of the past. Where contemporary science was challenging the authority of the biblical texts, Warren's archaeology was in the service of proving the accuracy of the biblical account. The seductive promise of archaeology is to show 'the glorious Temple standing'.

The excavation led by Professor Mazar started within weeks of the capture of Jerusalem in 1967. The area in front of the Western Wall had been cleared and made into a broad plaza for Jewish worship, which could not be a more marked symbolic gesture after the centuries of contention around the small pavement area that had been there. To dig around the Temple Mount itself was bound to be provocative, not least as it took place so soon after the end of the war. Protests came from all sides. The story of the progress of the dig is entertainingly told by Meir Ben-Dov. Ben-Dov was one of the archaeologists leading the excavation, so he is certainly not an impartial narrator (and his wry sense of humour and boundless self-confidence are bound to annoy his opponents), but his account of how the archaeologist deals with the vested interests that surround a dig in a politically sensitive area is eye-opening. The chief rabbi of the Sephardi (Spanish/Eastern) community, Rabbi Nissim, opposed the dig because he was afraid it might prove the Wailing Wall was not the western wall of the Temple Mount, and, in general, because anything that might challenge the faith of the faithful was to be prevented. (Muslim clerics argued this same general line.) The chief rabbi of the Ashkenazi (German/Western) community, Rabbi Unterman, had a more precise objection. The dig might uncover the Ark, which the *Midrash* claimed was buried beneath the Mount. The archaeologists thought that this would be the most wonderful discovery, but Rabbi Unterman's concern was that since the Temple was no more, no one could be ritually pure and so no one could touch the Ark. These oppositions held up the dig for a season.

Then Ben-Dov hit on a plan. The Jordanians had built a Muslim girls' school by the southern wall (despite the fact that it covered over fascinating remains of early Islamic Jerusalem). After the war, the school moved and the building had been slated for destruction. But the municipality had allowed the office of the Chief Rabbinate to use about half the rooms on a temporary basis. Ben-Dov sneakily arranged permission from the mayor to use some of the other rooms in the school and moved his equipment in. At the same time, despite the fact that the rabbis were still opposed to the dig, he staked out the territory and started excavation. When Rabbi Nissim saw some of the rooms of his building taken over, he was enraged. Soon the Minister of Religious Affairs and a string of local officials were beating down Ben-Dov's door to get him to vacate the rooms. A full-scale row broke out over the use of space in the school, and the honour of the rabbinate. Ben-Dov held his ground for a few days – while the dig got under way. By the time the issue of the rooms was settled, eighty archaeologists were on site, and the dig was a fait accompli.

Muslim clerics were also extremely sensitive about the politics of the excavation. What would the dig show about the early history of the Temple Mount and its ownership? Would it destroy Muslim relics in the search for Jewish ones? In their most extreme form, the complaint was that the Jews were trying to destroy the al-Aqsa Mosque. One of the first discoveries of the dig was an unknown Muslim palace, which revolutionised understanding of the early Muslim city. The deputy director of the Jordanian Department of Antiquities, Rafiq Dajani, visited the site. 'If we could leave politics to the politicians, I would heartily congratulate you on your work,'

33. An inscription, discovered during Professor Mazar's dig. It reads 'To the trumpet-call building to pr—,' and is probably from the Temple Mount, and may even be from the tower above the priests' house.

he said to Ben-Dov. 'The finds from the early Muslim period are thrilling, and frankly I am surprised that Israeli scholars have made them public.' His remarks were heard by a foreign correspondent, who published them. Dajani was sacked within a few days.

Ben-Dov is the hero of his own story, which is of the triumph of scientific inquiry over superstition and ignorance. Like Warren, he has to become involved with all the infighting of local and national politics and, like Warren, his own absolute commitment to the scientific pursuit of knowledge is a sword he wields against religious opposition. As with Warren, the results of the dig were stunning. The steps to the gates (Figure 14) and the stairway of Wilson's Arch (see Figure 13) are the grandest discoveries, but one of the most evocative is an inscription in Hebrew on a cornerstone from one of the towers of the walls that reads 'To the trumpet-call building to pr—' (Figure 33). Josephus says that a priest used to blow a trumpet from the tower above the priests' house to announce to the citizens the beginning and end of the Sabbath. This appears to be the dedication stone for the very spot from where this trumpet call was sounded.

⌛

The promise and the threat of archaeology is revelation of the buried past. The promise is to 'show the Temple standing'; the threat is to undermine the written accounts on which the Temple of the imagination has been built. The successes of the archaeologist are portrayed as heroic battles of discovery. It is harder to remember how much of archaeology is speculative inference. The archaeology of the Temple shows most beguilingly both the longing to recapture the real, insistent materiality of the past monument and the stories and fantasies which such longing also inevitably produces. Our image of the Temple is moulded by both forces.

II

THE TEMPLE AS MYTH:
FREEMASONS AND
THE KNIGHTS TEMPLAR

MASONIC MYSTERIES

Captain Warren was a passionate Freemason. Archaeologists do not usually mention this fact about their hero. He helped found the Quatuor Coronati Lodge of Masonic Research, dedicated to the history and archaeology of Freemasonry, for whom he read a paper on 'The Orientation of Temples', and he had close associations with a number of Lodges around the world. He rose to the highest levels of the organisation, which in the nineteenth century attracted many of the British establishment: the Grand Master of Britain, admitted in 1875 in a packed Albert Hall, was the Prince of Wales, later King Edward VII. The Temple is central to the myths and practices of Freemasonry. Warren's commitment to uncovering the topography of Jerusalem had more than one personal motivation.

The Freemasons came into being as a fully fledged organisation in the first quarter of the eighteenth century, and by the middle of the century had a fully established narrative of their own long history: a charter myth that goes back to the

Temple. The members subscribe to 'a peculiar system of morality, veiled in allegory and illustrated by symbols': both the allegory and the symbols are drawn from the Temple too. The mythic history of the Freemasons is an astoundingly naïve fiction which takes us back to the Book of Kings: 'King David began the Temple, called *Templum Domini*, now designated as the Temple of Jerusalem. This monarch constituted himself a patron of the Masons, and by every means in his power endeavoured to show how highly he prized them.' It is strange to see the medieval Latin name for the Dome of the Rock being taken as the original name of Solomon's Temple. The Temple was built, however, by 'Solomon's Masons', which shows, for the Freemason myth, the importance of their order's members in biblical times. One of the earliest recorded catechisms of the Scottish Freemasons asks, 'Where was the first Lodge?' and answers, 'In the Porch of Solomon's Temple', and one similar document makes Solomon the first Grandmaster of the Temple Lodge.

The most important hero of this Masonic myth is Hiram Abiff (sometimes referred to as H.A. in Masonic literature). Hiram Abiff is a name extracted somewhat awkwardly from the Book of Chronicles. When Solomon intended to build the Temple he sent to Huram, King of Tyre, for assistance. (In the Book of Kings, Huram is called Hiram, which adds to the confusion.) Huram sent Solomon 'a skilful and intelligent man, my master Huram'. The combination of this phrase in Chronicles and the name in Kings produces a hybrid, Hiram Abiff ('abiff' is a corruption of the Hebrew translated as 'my master'). This is the figure who is said to have been the master-builder of the Temple. In the myth, other craftsmen are desperate for his Masonic secrets, but

Hiram Abiff maintains a tight-lipped steadfastness. The other craftsmen murder him. Solomon orders the hunt that finds his dismembered body and uncovers the murderers. This myth is enacted as part of the initiation rites of modern Masonic Lodges. In American Lodges, initiated members play the role of the murderers and demand that the candidates reveal the secrets. The candidates refuse, and are ill-treated, before there is a search for the 'body', and the candidates are 'reborn' into membership of the Lodge.

The different levels of initiation also take their 'passwords' and allegorical meanings from the Temple. The first two levels are known as 'Boaz' and 'Jachin' after the two bronze pillars outside the porch of Solomon's Temple, cast, according to the Bible, by Hiram. The candidate for the first level who supplicates for entrance with the word of initiation receives the ritual reply: 'This word is derived from the left-hand pillar at the porchway or entrance of King Solomon's Temple, so-named after Boaz, the great-grandfather of David, a Prince and Ruler in Israel. The import of the word is "In strength". Pass, Boaz!' The allegorical guide round the Temple that is part of both *midrashic* and Christian exegesis has here become part of a new ritual to match the new myth of the Masons.

Leon Templo, whose models of the Temple were influential at about the time that Freemasonry was becoming established as an organisation, was said to have been one of the earliest Jewish members of a Masonic Lodge. His model of the Temple was visited by Lawrence Dermott, one of the founding fathers of Freemasonry. Dermott was fascinated by any account of 'the most memorable thinges in the Tabernacle of Moses and the Temple of Salaomon, according to the text of scripture'. Dermott, Masonic Grand Secretary, consequently adopted the coat of arms of Leon Templo for the coat of arms of his Lodge. It is a bizarre quirk of the history of the Temple that the coat of arms of a Dutch Jew, made famous for his model of the Temple, should have been redrawn as the coat of arms of a Masonic Lodge, a new mythic rebuilding of the Temple.

Freemasonry has often been the object of suspicion and derision for its secret rituals. The most virulent attack comes from two Muslim academics, who state that it was founded by Jews in the first century, was instrumental in the foundation of communism, Nazism and Zionism, and 'strives … to spread sexual anarchism and moral disintegration'. The intimate link between American imperialism and Freemasonry can be seen on the dollar bill: 'a close look at the US Dollar would reveal the first letter of the word Zion engraved between the two pillars of Boas and Jikin'. Its ultimate aim is to rebuild a Temple on top of the al-Aqsa Mosque. Such paranoid ranting in the guise of scholarly research is horrible, but it is also a grimly distorted mirror of the myths of the Temple that the Freemasons provide. They do seek roots in ancient history and authority from the Bible, and, above all, for Freemasons the dominant idea that links the myth, rituals and even the buildings of the organisation is precisely the idea of building a new Temple – though not on the al-Aqsa. Different and competing myths of rebuilding the Temple become easily and dangerously intertwined with religious and political fanaticism.

The Knights Templar did take over the mosque and turned it into a church of Christianity. They lived on the Temple Mount and were famous for their violent guarding of the roads to Jerusalem. They were an international Order of Christian warriors who came together during the Crusades to fight for Christendom against the infidel. St Bernard, contemporary with the Order's beginning, gives us the most extraordinary version of the mission of the Crusades: they were 'unbelieving scoundrels, sacrilegious plunderers, homicides, perjurers, adulterers, whose departure from Europe is certainly a double benefit, seeing that people in Europe are glad to see the back of them, and the people to whose assistance they are going in the Holy Land are delighted to see them'. He gave the expedition his blessing with what seems a baffling version of a saintly message: the Knights Templar kill without sin and for a glorious reward, he declared, because they fight for Christ. 'The soldier of Christ kills safely; he dies the more safely.' With this religious carte-blanche, the reputation of the Knights Templar among the Muslims for awful cruelty seems unsurprising.

They were harsh to each other too. When Adam de Valaincourt left the brotherhood and then returned, he was compelled to eat with dogs on the floor for a year, to fast on bread and water three days a week and to appear naked every Sunday at the altar for scourging. But there was great Christian support for the Templars and they received gifts of large and valuable tracts of land. Their international connections also enabled them to act as bankers as well as a small military elite. It was because of this financial success, at least in part, that the Order was banned in 1314 by Philip IV of

France, who had its leaders killed and its properties confiscated. The weak Pope Clement V did nothing to stop the king of France's appropriation of Templar wealth.

The Order may have been banned, but it returned in full flower centuries later, invested with swathes of Romantic gloss. The Knights Templar are features of the medieval fantasies of Sir Walter Scott and his ilk, as a pure, secret band of brothers, Knights of Christ. They haunt the woods of Gothic fiction. 'The cruelty and oppression of the Turkomans ... aroused the religious chivalry of Christendom,' begins one archetypal mid-Victorian history, whose author presumably had not read St Bernard's judgement. Groups of young men, 'hankering after romanticized social prestige', actually started to form groups of Templars, especially in Germany, where it suited to see the Crusaders as 'religious and warlike princes who wished to enlighten, edify and build up living Temples of the Most High'. They acted out jousts and knights' expeditions (till in one case contact with a real army led to ignominious flight). These groups often overlapped with the Freemasons, and the higher degree of initiation into the Masons became based on the myth of the knights. As early as 1672 Elias Ashmole, founding benefactor of the Ashmolean Museum in Oxford and a keen Freemason, called the Knights Templar 'the principal columns which supported the Kingdom of Jerusalem'. The medieval knights who terrorised the roads of Palestine are a far cry from the chivalrous princes of Romantic fiction, but both share in the same fantasy of 'building up the living Temple'.

There is a fine medieval church in London built by the Knights Templar, near the underground station called Temple. When the Order was banned in the fourteenth century, the so-called Temple Church and the surrounding buildings were taken over by lawyers, and this is where the Inner Temple and the Middle Temple, the Inns of Court where barristers meet and dine, still are today. The Temple Church marked the boundary between the City of London and the City of Westminster, and was known as the 'Barrière du Temple' – Temple Bar: because lawyers frequented the spot they were known as 'barristers'. When Allenby walked into Jerusalem in 1917, the barristers held a special ceremony in the Temple Church. They processed around the church and placed laurel wreathes on the effigies of the knights buried there. A Christian army, the first since 1239, had returned to Jerusalem.

The sermon was delivered by E. W. Barnes, a mathematician and cleric. As the Bishop of Birmingham, he delivered famous addresses known as '"gorilla" sermons' which defended the theory of human evolution and involved him in a series of post-Darwinian theological spats. (In the 1920s there were public protests against his attempts to make religion more scientific.) This special service was planned, he declared, so 'that we may with grave humility rededicate our arms to God' – as Christian soldiers. 'We cannot meditate upon the capture of Jerusalem,' he continued, 'without thinking of that Great Order, splendid in its inception, dramatic in its fall, to which we owe this splendid building.' This meditation indeed led into an extended and glorifying history of the Knights Templar and their fight for a Christian Jerusalem, which culminated in the present triumph of their aim: 'Once again the object of the Crusades is accomplished and the Holy Sepulchre is under Christian control.' Barnes concluded by reminding the congregants of 'the solemn and awful responsibility of Empire' before they all sang the hymns 'Zion's King Shall Reign Supreme' and, perhaps inevitably, 'Gird on Thy Conquering Sword'.

It is not easy for a modern audience simply to enjoy this rhetoric of empire, but what most sharply indicates our current distance from his ideological position is the fact that Barnes was a notable pacifist (not something easy to be in 1917), a position which 'failed to endear him' to his more bellicose colleagues. But this sermon at least clearly hit the mark. As one friend noted, he had 'a challenging incisiveness and evident, if somewhat naïve, intellectual honesty which his congregation of able lawyers could appreciate'. The Choir Committee of the Temple voted at its meeting of 18 December 1917 to print 300 copies of the sermon to be distributed to the Masters of the Bench of the Inner and the Middle Temple.

It is hard to appreciate all the layers, ironies and difficulties of such a ceremony in such a place at such a date with such a speaker and audience – but it does seem a perfect example of just how intricate and bizarre the myth of the Temple can turn out to be.

12

THE TEMPLE IS OURS!

The story of the capture of Jerusalem in 1967 is one that all Israelis know. Motta Gur, later Israeli Chief of Staff, looked down over the city, grabbed the microphone of the signal transmitter of his jeep and gave his brief speech to the troops: 'The Temple Mount, the Western Wall, the Old City. For 2,000 years our people have prayed for this moment. Let us go forward to victory.' The troops drove on, and soon he sent his famous message to the HQ Central Command: 'The Temple Mount is ours: repeat, the Temple Mount is ours!' As the soldiers fought through the streets and alleys, a paratrooper yelled, 'The Western Wall! I can see the Wall,' and from the Temple Mount and elsewhere his comrades rushed down to join him. They had fought for thirty-two hours, and now they leant against the wall, wept and prayed.

It need not be emphasised that this is a story from the point of view of the victors. How it is read will depend on the politics of the reader. What is equally telling, however, is how the capture of the Temple Mount, the site of Solomon's Temple and Herod's Temple, leads to prayer at the Wailing Wall. The soldiers – and the story – find emotional release at the outside wall of the platform of the Temple. Two thousand years of history have worked their force on the imagination: for centuries the only spot the Jews could reach was this pavement outside the Temple Mount. It had become so full of religious awe and yearning that it was the one place truly to excite the feelings of the soldiers and, indeed, the feelings of hundreds of thousands of Jews who have visited the site since. This is not just because for most orthodox Jews it is against religious law either to go on to the Temple Mount or to try to rebuild the Temple before the Messiah comes. It is a paradigm of how the Temple must always be a monument of the imagination. Over history and in history it is always being reconstructed, replaced, repictured.

Because the Temple Mount is so charged a religious site, the wars that have been fought for it make every fight more than a battle for control. The Temple is so tied up with a view of the world that every struggle to possess it expresses a view of one's place in history: an act of self-definition in the order of things. It also expresses a view of the divine, of messianism and of the religious in the order of things. It becomes the object of myth, fantasy and political idealism.

It is because the Temple has mattered so profoundly in this way that generations of thinkers, artists and theologians have struggled to create an image of it. These images in words, in pictures and in models are the product of individuals who inhabit particular eras and particular cultural milieus: they are acts of personal creation that also show how every attempt to think about the Temple, including my own, is of its time. Where the Temple is concerned, we are all slaves of history. These images live long in the mind, and are fully part of how the Temple is conceived. They too are part of the archaeology of the Temple.

Nor is there any sign of this intense valorisation of the Temple ceasing. Doctors in Jerusalem are familiar with what they now call 'Jerusalem syndrome' – a religious madness which comes to a head in the shadow of the Temple Mount. An Australian tourist, a non-Jew, Michael Rohan, set fire to the al-Aqsa Mosque in 1969 because he was 'the Lord's Emissary', as predicted in the Book of Zechariah (that's what he told the court on his way to the hospital for the criminally insane). An Israeli soldier, Allen Goodman, went on a shooting rampage in the al-Aqsa Mosque too, because he hoped to become 'King of the Jews by liberating this Holy Spot'.

Unfortunately, the problem is not just an issue of the occasional psychotic individual. There are also small, obsessional groups, fed by a mixture of political and religious intensity, which have been established with the aim of reclaiming the Temple Mount in order to build a new Temple. These groups, such as the 'Jerusalem Temple Foundation', or the 'Temple Institute', or the 'Temple Mount and Land of Israel Faithful Movement', are in constant battle with the state and the courts of Israel, and inevitably see themselves as the one true hope. As with all such movements, there are earnest policy statements, papers on aims and objectives, and paranoid tales of heroism and a messianic future. There are two Talmud schools where scholars are being trained in the rituals of the priesthood for when this new Temple is built. Two rabbis, Yehuda Getz and Shlomo Goren, have claimed to know where the Ark is buried and to have seen the place in a clandestine dig (which has produced a frenzy of internet discussion by similarly committed groups).

Extreme evangelical Christians, particularly in America, help fund these organisations and share some of their more unpleasant traits. Muslims have responded with matching paranoia (there are stories that circulate that the stones have been already cut for the new Temple and the cedars from Lebanon prepared), and there have been riots (since the 1930s at least) that are part and parcel of the current tensions in the city and region. 'Jerusalem syndrome' all too quickly becomes a shared malady.

The Temple remains a symbol that goes to the heart of current Middle Eastern politics and is as bitterly contested now in the twenty-first century as at any point in its long history. It is a contest that involves archaeologists as much as soldiers, theologians as much as politicians, artists as much as zealots – the passionate and the casual, the thoughtful and the unthinking, the foolish and the wise. Everyone has a stake in the Temple. But it is always worth asking who is included and who is excluded when someone declares, 'The Temple is ours!'

⬛

The Temple encapsulates why a building can be so much more than an architectural design. To engage with the Temple is to engage with a long history of longing and grief, fantasy and power, artistic dreams and political machina-tions. The Temple may have no physical existence, but it fully embodies what is meant by a Great Building of the World.

MAKING A VISIT ?

There is no Temple to see, of course, but the Temple Mount and the Western Wall, as I write, are open for visitors. Of the other sites and sights:

- The Temple Scroll can be seen in the Israel Museum in Jerusalem.
- The Dura-Europos panels can be seen in Damascus Museum, Damascus.
- Schott's model is preserved in the Museum für Hamburgische Geschichte in Hamburg.
- Some of Schick's models can be seen in the St Paulus Hospital, known as Schick's School, opposite the Damascus Gate in Jerusalem.
- Bernini's Baldacchino is a standard for visitors to Rome, as is the Arch of Titus.
- Alec Garrard's model of the Temple is now in transition between sites: he can be contacted at Moat Farm, Fressingfield, Eye, Suffolk IP21 5TB.
- The Temple Church in London is open to visitors (tube: Temple).

FURTHER READING

CHAPTER 1: A MONUMENT OF THE IMAGINATION

There is no book that covers the range of the present volume. A good introduction to the architectural heritage of the Temple is Helen Rosenau, *Vision of the Temple: The Image of the Temple of Jerusalem in Judaism and Christianity* (London, 1979); a clear, nicely illustrated but rather simplified account of the history of the Temple Mount is to be found in Joan Comay, *The Temple of Jerusalem with a History of the Temple Mount* (London, 1975); a good older introductory volume to the Temple in general is A. Parrot, *The Temple of Jerusalem* (London, 1957).

CHAPTERS 2 AND 3:
SOLOMON'S TEMPLE AND ITS REBUILDING

Translations from the Book of Kings are taken largely from the Jewish Publication Society version. The *Midrash* are wonderfully collected and translated in L. Ginzberg, *The Legends of the Jews* (7 vols), trans. H. Szold (Philadelphia, 1913–36). The translation of *Midrash Eicha Rabbah* is taken from the Soncino edition of the *Midrash Rabbah* under the general editorship of H. Freedman and M. Simon (London and New York, 1983). The story of the Temple Scroll is told

[176]

with real verve by Yigael Yadin, *The Temple Scroll* (Jerusalem, 1985) and the whole can be reviewed in his three-volume work, also titled *The Temple Scroll* (Jerusalem, 1983); on the Dead Sea Scrolls see G. Vermes, *The Dead Sea Scrolls: Qumran in Perspective* (London, 1994), and H. Shanks (ed.), *Understanding the Dead Sea Scrolls* (New York, 1992). There is a fine discussion of the archaeological and historical background to this period in Adolfo Roitman, *Envisioning the Temple* (Jerusalem, 2003). For Bernini and St Peter's, see Irving Lavin, *Bernini and the Crossing of St Peter's* (New York, 1968).

CHAPTER 4: HEROD'S TEMPLE

The best historical background is to be found in Seth Schwartz, *Imperialism and Jewish Society 200 BCE, to 640 CE* (Princeton, 2001); Elias Bickerman, *The Jews in the Greek Age* (Cambridge, Mass., 1988) is insightful on the relation between Jews and the dominant culture of the Mediterranean, as is the classic work of Martin Hengel, *Judaism and Hellenism*, II vols (Philadelphia, 1974). A range of approaches is also on show in J. Lieu, J. North and T. Rajak (eds), *Jews among Pagans and Christians in the Roman Empire* (London, 1992). On the archaeology, see Leon and Kathleen Ritmeyer, *Secrets of Jerusalem's Temple Mount* (Washington, DC, 1988); a massive German compilation of all the available information is Th. Busink, *Die Tempel von Jerusalem von Salomon bis Herodes*, 2 vols (Leiden, 1970–80); most lively, however, is Meir Ben-Dov, *In the Shadow of the Temple* (Jerusalem and New York, 1985), which gives a dramatic account of the digs as well as their results. J. Wilkinson, *Jerusalem as Jesus Knew*

It: Archaeology as Evidence (London, 1978), is a clear introduction to the archaeological issues, within a wider frame. On the religious services, see Menahen Haran, *Temples and Temple Service in Ancient Israel* (Oxford, 1978) and Francis Schmidt, *How the Temple Thinks: Identity and Social Cohesion in Ancient Judaism*, trans. J. E. Crawley (Shefield, 2001). For non-biblical sources on the Temple, a useful source book is C. Hayward, *The Jewish Temple: a Non-Biblical Source Book* (London and New York, 1996), which translates and discusses passages from Josephus and Philo among others.

CHAPTER 5: THE TEMPLE OF THE SCHOLARS

The translations of tractate 'Middoth' are taken from the Soncino edition of the Babylonian Talmud. An excellent introduction to the Talmud is Adin Steinsaltz, *The Essential Talmud* (London, 1976). A lively, influential but perhaps unreliable discussion of the Talmud's argumentation is to be found in Susan Handelman's *The Slayers of Moses: The Emergence of Rabbinic Interpretation in Modern Literary Theory* (Albany, 1982); much sounder and even more provocative is Daniel Boyarin, *Intertextuality and the Reading of Midrash* (Bloomington, 1990); more sober is Louis Jacobs's *Structure and Form in the Babylonian Talmud* (Cambridge, 1991).

CHAPTER 6: YOUR BODY IS A TEMPLE

For general background see Robin Lane Fox, *Pagans and Christians* (London, 1986), and, for a somewhat wackier account, Keith Hopkins, *A World Full of Gods: Pagans, Jews* and *Christians in the Roman Empire* (London, 1999). Joachim Jeremias, *Jerusalem in the Time of Jesus* (London, 1969), is also insightful on the role of the Temple in Jerusalem. On St Paul, I have a soft spot for Daniel Boyarin's *A Radical Jew: Paul and the Politics of Identity* (Berkeley, 1994). Robert Gundry, in *Soma in Biblical Theology, with an Emphasis on Pauline Anthropology* (Cambridge, 1976), lays out the theological issues of the body clearly, though Peter Brown's *The Body and Society: Men, Women and Sexual Renunciation in Early Christianity* (New York, 1988) is an essential guide to the overall issue of body politics. L. Gaston, *No Stone on Another* (Leiden, 1970), and C. Grappe, *D'un Temple à l'autre* (Paris, 1992), discuss the transition from Jewish to Christian Temple. J. Wilkinson, *Jerusalem Pilgrims Before the Crusades* (Warminster, 1977), collects and translates early Christian travellers' accounts which reveal their studied indifference to the Temple Mount. On Anicia Juliana see Martin Harrison, *A Temple for Byzantium* (Austin, Texas, 1989); on Hagia Sophia a standard introduction is Rowland Mainstone, *Hagia Sophia* (London, 1988). For early modern use of the Temple, see Jim Bennett and Scott Mandlebrote, *The Garden, the Ark, the Tower, the Temple* (Oxford, 1998), and for the idea that Salisbury Cathedral and many other buildings are constructed according to the ratios of Ezekiel's Temple see J. Wilkinson, *From Synagogue to Church* (London, 2000), who is more extreme in its pursuit of ratios than Harrison. The quotation from Ernst Lohmeyer is taken from his *Lord of the Temple* (Edinburgh and London, 1961), originally published in German in 1942.

CHAPTER 7: CALIPHS AND CRUSADERS

Al-Muqaddasi is translated by B. Collins, *The Best Divisions for Knowledge of the Regions* (Reading, 2001); the translation of the Qur'an is taken from Arthur Arberry's version for the Oxford World Classics series (Oxford, 1964); *The Life of the Prophet Mohammed: Al-Sira al-Nabawiyya* is translated by Trevor Le Gassick (Reading, 1998); and a more general source book is Norman Calder, Jawid Mojaddedi and Andrew Rippin, *Classical Islam: A Sourcebook of Religious Literature* (London and New York, 2003). Gerhard Endress, *Islam: An Historical Introduction*, 2nd edn (Edinburgh, 2002), and Jonathan Berkey, *The Formation of Islam: Religion and Society in the Near East, 600–1800* (Cambridge, 2003), are good introductions to the historical issues, while Chase Robinson, *Islamic Historiography* (Cambridge, 2003), is excellent on the problems of the source material. The one essential book on the Temple Mount is Said Nuseibeh and Oleg Grabar's *The Dome of the Rock* (London, 1996), which contains splendid pictures as well as a good commentary. A. Maalouf, *The Crusades Through Arab Eyes* (London, 1984), or, even better, Carole Hillenbrand, *Crusades: Islamic Perspectives* (New York, 1999), give a necessary corrective to romantic fantasies about the Crusaders. Jonathan Riley-Smith (ed.), *The Oxford History of the Crusades* (Oxford, 1999), is a good starting point for this period.

CHAPTER 8: THE ARTIST'S EYE

The main pictures here are from these works: Juan Bautista Villalpando, *In Ezechielem Explanationes*, 3 vols (Rome, 1594–1605); Conrad Schick, *Die Stiftshütte, der Tempel in*

Jerusalem und der Tempelplatz der Jetztzeit (Berlin, 1896); James Fergusson, *The Temple of the Jews* (London, 1878); Carl Watzinger, *Denkmäler Palästinas*, 2 vols (Leipzig, 1933). Leon Templo's illustrations can be found in Jacob Judah Leon, *Retrato del Templo de Selomoh* (Middelburg, 1642), and for the story see A. K. Offenberg, 'Jacob Jehudah Leon (1602–1675) and his model of the Temple', in J. van den Borg and E. van der Wall (eds.), *Jewish–Christian Relations in the Seventeenth Century* (Dardrecht, 1988). On Fergusson's Indian scholarship, a simple introduction can be found in Colin Cunningham, 'James Fergusson's History of Indian Architecture', in Catherine King (ed.), *Views of Difference, Different Views of Art* (New Haven, 1999). Alec Garrard has privately published *The Spendour of the Temple* (Eye, 1997), which fully illustrates his model.

CHAPTER 9: TRAVELLERS' TALES

James Buzard, *The Beaten Track: European Tourism, Literature and the Ways to 'Culture'* (Oxford, 1993), and Mary Campbell, *The Witness and the Other World: Exotic European Travel Writing, 400–1600* (Ithaca, NY, 1988), both give good introductions to the background here. 'The Itinerary of a Certain Englishman' can be found in E. Hoade, *Western Pilgrims* (Jerusalem, 1952). A. W. Kinglake's *Eothen* went through many editions from its first publication in 1847, and is one of the few of these volumes still in print; Harriet Martineau's *Eastern Life: Present and Past*, 3 vols (London, 1848) is a fascinating example of an influential account of such travel by a woman who became famous in other spheres too. Robert

Richardson, *Travels along the Mediterranean and Parts Adjacent*, 2 vols (London, 1822), is a paradigm of the genre.

CHAPTER 10: ARCHAEOLOGY AND IMPERIALISM

On Captain Charles Warren, see his *Underground Jerusalem* (London, 1876) and *The Temple of the Jews* (London, 1880), a rebuttal of James Fergusson's *The Temple of the Jews* (London, 1878). W. W. Williams, *The Life of General Sir Charles Warren* (Oxford, 1941) is a wonderful account of a Victorian hero. Meir Ben-Dov, *In the Shadow of the Temple* (Jerusalem and New York, 1985), tells the story of Mazar's dig. A full picture of the underground cisterns and chambers of the Temple Mount can be found in Shimon Gibson and David Jacobsen, *Below the Temple Mount in Jerusalem* (Oxford, 1996).

CHAPTER 11: FREEMASONS AND KNIGHTS TEMPLAR

On the Freemasons see James Dewar, *The Unlocked Secret: Freemasonry Examined* (London, 1966); R. Wells, *Understanding Freemasonry* (London, 1991); Alexander Horne, *King Solomon's Temple in the Masonic Tradition* (Wellingborough, 1972); J. S. M. Ward, *Freemasonry and the Ancient Gods* (London, 1921). The Arab extremist version is Muhammed Safwat al-Saqua Amini and Sa'di Abu Habib, *Freemasonry* (New York, 1982). On the Knights Templar see Peter Partner, *The Murdered Magicians: The Templars and Their Myth* (Oxford, 1981). For an example of history as romance you couldn't do better than C. G. Addison, *The History of the Knights Templar, the Temple Church and the*

Temple (London, 1842). Barnes's sermon was privately published (in 1918) as 'Jerusalem: A Sermon Preached in Commemoration of the Capture of Jerusalem on Sunday, December 16th, 1917 at the Temple Church'.

LIST OF ILLUSTRATIONS

ENDPAPERS

'Jerusalem from the Mount of Olives', lithograph by Louis Haghe after David Roberts, 1887

ILLUSTRATION CREDITS

Alinari Archive, Florence: 1; Alec Garrard: 31; *Guardian*, © Don McPhee: 3; HarperCollins Publishers, Inc.: 14; Weidenfeld & Nicolson, a division of the Orion Publishing Group: 9, 10.

While every effort has been made to contact copyright-holders of illustrations, the author and publishers would be grateful for information about any illustrations where they have been unable to trace them, and would be glad to make amendments in further editions.

DATING SCHEMES
AND TRANSLATIONS

Ancient Greeks and Romans, and modern Jews, Christians and Muslims all use different dating schemes. This book is about all of these cultures. I had to decide whether to use several different systems (Muslim dating for the Muslim chapters and so on), or to use one system for clarity. Any answer is an ideological minefield, and I am well aware of the issues. I have used BC and AD – the Christian system – because it is most familiar to most readers, despite the fact that this might look like acquiescence to one dominant culture. I was finally persuaded not to use CE and BCE when I was asked by a baffled group of museum visitors what the letters meant and why were they used.

Translation from sacred texts is always an issue. Translations from Latin, Greek and modern languages (French, German, Italian) are my own, except where indicated. The translations from the Hebrew Bible, from Aramaic and Hebrew sources and the Arabic materials are from standard English versions, which are listed in the Further Reading section.

ACKNOWLEDGEMENTS

This book has been great fun to write, even when my friends have forced me into a steep learning curve. Thanks to Stefan Reif, Basim Musallam, Robin Cormack and Helen Morales, who read and commented and advised. And a special thanks to Seth Schwartz, for years of sardonic correction, and to Diana Lipton, running and talking partner. Mary Beard's editing was, as ever, spot on.

INDEX

Hiram Abiff (master builder) 29, 164–5
Hiram (Huram), King of Tyre 25, 29, 164
Holford, George 106
Holy of Holies 26, 28, 31, 61, 70–71, 77, 79, 146
House of the Name of the Lord God (*hamakom*) *see* Solomon's Temple

I

Isaac 92
Ishaq, Ibn 112
Islam 11–14, 16, 109–19
Israel, State of 14

J

Jachin and Boaz 29, 165, 166
Jacob 92
Jebusites 20
Jeremiah 42
Jeremiah, Book of 33
Jerome, St 103, 143
Jerusalem 20, 58, 81, 109–10, 143–51, 171
'Jerusalem syndrome' 173, 174
Jesus 9–10, 99–100, 109
Jews *see* Judaism
John, Gospel of 10, 99

Jonathan 19
Josephus 1–2, 17, 58–9, 60, 66, 67, 71–2, 98, 130, 136, 161
Josiah, King 24
Judaea 1, 48, 81, 82
Judaism 1, 11, 12, 14, 16, 20, 47–54, 72–80, 86–95
    festivals 48–51
Julian the Apostate 84–6
Juliana, Ancia 104
Jupiter, temple to 81
Justinian, Emperor 104–5

K

Kinglake, A. W. 150
Kings, Book of 8, 19–41, 47, 164
Knights Templar 12, 122, 167–70

L

Lailat al Miraj 113
Lamentations, Book of 33, 39
Lamy, Bernard 125, 128
Lebanon Forest House 30
Leon, Jacob Judah (Leon Templo) 138–40, 165–6
Lohmeyer, Ernst 107

WONDERS OF THE WORLD

This is a small series of books, under the general editorship of Mary Beard, that will focus on some of the world's most famous sites or monuments.

Already available

Mary Beard: *The Parthenon*
Robert Irwin: *The Alhambra*
Richard Jenkyns: *Westminster Abbey*